Creative Health for Pianists

Creative Health for Pianists

CONCEPTS, EXERCISES & COMPOSITIONS

Pedro de Alcantara

Oxford University Press is a department of the University of Oxford. It furthers the University's objective of excellence in research, scholarship, and education by publishing worldwide. Oxford is a registered trade mark of Oxford University Press in the UK and certain other countries.

Published in the United States of America by Oxford University Press
198 Madison Avenue, New York, NY 10016, United States of America.

© Oxford University Press 2023

All rights reserved. No part of this publication may be reproduced, stored in a retrieval system, or transmitted, in any form or by any means, without the prior permission in writing of Oxford University Press, or as expressly permitted by law, by license, or under terms agreed with the appropriate reproduction rights organization. Inquiries concerning reproduction outside the scope of the above should be sent to the Rights Department, Oxford University Press, at the address above.

You must not circulate this work in any other form
and you must impose this same condition on any acquirer.

Library of Congress Cataloging-in-Publication Data
Names: Alcantara, Pedro de, 1958– author.
Title: Creative health for pianists : concepts, exercises & compositions / Pedro de Alcantara.
Description: New York : Oxford University Press, 2023. |
Includes bibliographical references and index.
Identifiers: LCCN 2022053637 (print) | LCCN 2022053638 (ebook) |
ISBN 9780197600214 (paperback) | ISBN 9780197600207 (hardback) | ISBN 9780197600238 (epub)
Subjects: LCSH: Piano—Methods.
Classification: LCC MT222.A47 2023 (print) | LCC MT222 (ebook) |
DDC 786.2/193—dc23/eng/20221103
LC record available at https://lccn.loc.gov/2022053637
LC ebook record available at https://lccn.loc.gov/2022053638

DOI: 10.1093/oso/9780197600207.001.0001

To Alexandre Mion

Contents

List of Figures · ix

List of Photo Credits · xi

Preface · xiii

Acknowledgments · xxi

About the Companion Website · xxiii

Introduction · 1

1 Dialogue · 9

2 Heartbreak · 43

3 Seesaw · 85

4 Celeste · 104

5 The Circle · 147

6 Gesture · 182

7 Advanced Seesaw · 208

8 Sonic Play · 254

9 Horn Call · 297

10 Mudra · 331

Conclusion · 363

Appendix: Practicing the Circle of Fifths · 365

Resources · 385

Index · 393

Figures

Preface

Figure 0.1 Discovery xix

Chapter 3

Figure 3.1 Bouncing 95
Figure 3.2 Bouncing, too 95

Chapter 4

Figure 4.1 Struggle 108
Figure 4.2 Gradations 109
Figure 4.3 Oscillations 111

Chapter 5

Figure 5.1 The circle of fifths 149
Figure 5.2 The manifold circle of fifths 151
Figure 5.3 The cathedral at Chartres 154
Figure 5.4 Layers of the keyboard 165
Figure 5.5 Count Basie 181

Chapter 6

Figure 6.1 Left and right 192
Figure 6.2 Nested hands 200
Figure 6.3 The growth of hands 203

Chapter 7

Figure 7.1 Hands at the party 210

Chapter 8

Figure 8.1 Architect and composer 262

Chapter 9

Figure 9.1 The Horn Call 303

Chapter 10

Figure 10.1   Mudra   332
Figure 10.2   The master and the learner   333

Conclusion

Figure C.1   Propagation   364

Photo Credits

Figure 0.1	Discovery. © Everett Collection	Shutterstock.	xix
Figure 3.1	Bouncing. © OryPhotography	Shutterstock.	95
Figure 3.2	Bouncing, too. © CroMary	Shutterstock.	95
Figure 4.1	Struggle. © lapina	Shutterstock.	108
Figure 4.2	Gradations. © Social Media Hub	Shutterstock.	109
Figure 4.3	Oscillations. © Pedro de Alcantara.	111
Figure 5.1	The circle of fifths. © Pedro de Alcantara.	149
Figure 5.2	The manifold circle of fifths. © Pedro de Alcantara.	151
Figure 5.3	The cathedral at Chartres. © Christian Musat	Shutterstock.	154
Figure 5.4	Layers of the keyboard. © Pedro de Alcantara.	165
Figure 5.5	Count Basie. © Olga Popova	Shutterstock.	181
Figure 6.1	Left and right. © sportpoint	Shutterstock.	192
Figure 6.2	Nested hands. © Alexis Niki & Pedro de Alcantara.	200
Figure 6.3	The growth of hands. © Yashkin Ilya	Shutterstock.	203
Figure 7.1	Hands at the party. © Vladimir Borovic, Montira Areepongthum, Africa Studio	Shutterstock.	210
Figure 8.1	Architect and composer. © sirtravelalot	Shutterstock.	262
Figure 9.1	The Horn Call. © kokrabue	Shutterstock.	303
Figure 10.1	Mudra. © Dmitry Rukhlenko	Shutterstock.	332
Figure 10.2	The master and the learner. © Beatrice Sirinuntananon, William Bank Wongveerakul	Shutterstock.	333
Figure C.1	Propagation. © Pedro de Alcantara.	364

Preface

Is This Method for You?

A paradigm is a set of principles and beliefs, preferences and hierarchies: "To me, *this* is important and *that* isn't important." Your paradigm as a musician determines your practice habits, your aesthetics, your relationship with the printed score, your career choices, and much more besides. Your paradigm is your operating system, the stuff you live by.

In *Creative Health for Musicians* I propose a new paradigm—in other words, a shift in what is important. The paradigm starts with broad definitions. I believe that a *musician* is anyone who's engaged with the materials of music, its sensorial aspects, its structures and mysteries. A little child who sings "Twinkle Twinkle Little Star" to herself is a musician, because in her own way she's engaged with the materials and mysteries of music. I define *creativity* broadly, too. I see it as the quality of your presence in the world, a combination of curiosity, attentiveness, and adaptability. By virtue of being alive you're already creative, but you can improve your creativity by becoming more curious, attentive, and adaptable. I also define *health* broadly. Like creativity, your health is your overall response to the world, a constantly changing state of being in which you see, hear, feel, think, and decide what you're going to do today, tomorrow, and the day after. Good health is a creative act.

Broadening your definitions broadens your pianistic and musical mind. A four-step procedure then allows you to put the paradigm to work. You can take these steps sequentially, one after the other—or simultaneously, as an integrated approach to everything that you do.

1. Start by paying a little extra attention to the world around you.
2. Acknowledge your own existence as a human being capable of agency.
3. Meet a creative stimulus or situation.
4. Fashion your creative response to the creative stimulus.

The world around you is architecture and art, weather, shapes and colors, laughter, friendship, and love. Your piano was designed in Japan and built in Indonesia, and it was shipped to your home in Paris thanks to an incredibly intricate supply chain. A Yamaha upright encapsulates several centuries in the history of music and, by extension, the history of humanity itself. Before you strike a note, you ponder the unfathomable web of connections leading to this moment in which you'll play something that Johann Sebastian Bach composed three hundred years ago. Wonderment and gratitude become a habit that you can tend to—and, in my opinion, that you *should* tend to.

It's you sitting at the piano now: not J. S. Bach, not your music teacher, not your parents nor your siblings. And it's you who's going to decide what you're going to do, why, and how. You'll need to take into account your goals, your strengths and weaknesses, your hopes and fears. Every sound you make at the piano comes from the interaction of these inner factors.

Inescapably, "working on the piano" is "working on yourself." It's another habit that you can tend to . . . and, in my opinion, that you *should* tend to.

At the piano, you'll face an endless flow of creative situations. Two notes, a chord, a melody; a novelty, a difficulty, something you don't understand, or something you know for sure that you don't like. Sharps and flats, counting, the coordination of left and right hands, an impossibly difficult score, a composition that seems pointless. An invitation to embellish, vary, or improvise a passage. An interdiction, which may come from a teacher or from a score or from your own mind. Don't sound too good, or people will notice you! Play better, or people will judge you! The creative flow never stops, and this is why you need to keep "working on yourself" non-stop, too.

When musicians talk about technique, they sometimes mean *a physical solution to a physical problem*. This has its merits, but in my paradigm I see technique as *a creative response to a creative situation*. Head, neck, back, legs, and feet; shoulders, arms, wrists, hands, and fingers; your orientation in space and your sense of time: they're all pertinent to the process. Ultimately, your intentions and perceptions give rise to the gestures that produce sound. The physicality of technique can't be isolated from your creative intentionality.

Metaphysics ("the mysteries of the world"), psychology ("the mysteries of my existence"), and creativity ("the mysteries of music") all precede technique ("the mysteries of embodiment"). When you put technique ahead of the rest, you play in a certain way. When you respect the hierarchy of mysteries, you play in a different way. This is the paradigm shift that *Creative Health for Pianists* invites you to explore.

Many of my compositions are simple on purpose. In order to respect the hierarchy of mysteries, it's useful to tackle streamlined compositions without too many things going on, so that you can really pay attention and make choices. Behind their plain façade, however, my compositions hide a wealth of sounds and sensations to be explored: the perception of vibration, for instance, or the ambiguity of intervals that make you happy and sad at the same time. Or, more importantly, how you really feel about yourself, about the piano, and about music.

Creative Health for Pianists has its share of analytical tools, its share of delights for musicians who enjoy involvement, discipline, and homework. For instance, throughout the book I share sequences of compositions that get more complicated little by little. Sometimes a complication arises suddenly, and this too I do on purpose, inviting you to make decisions. "Am I threatened by this difficulty, or do I find it stimulating? Do I play it, or do I skip it? Do I play it as written, or do I tweak it? Do I get bored, or do I get annoyed?" Questions like this are normal in everyone's daily lives, but I bring them to the fore as part of the learning process, so that you can "work on yourself" and refine your decision-making skills.

Creative Health for Pianists is a tool. You can use it in a lot of different ways, including as a companion or foil to other methods that may be more technique-oriented, and as a preliminary to compositions more elaborate than the ones I offer. In fact, you can use it in any way you want.

What does the book contain?

- Suggestions regarding general posture, the hands' stability at the keyboard, a sensitive touch with many gradations of strength, and the development of healthy gestures that come from a healthy attitude toward musical and instrumental exploration.

- Psychological concepts such as non-doing, non-judgment, and the constructive observation of your own frame of mind as you're confronted with situations and challenges.
- Exercises presented as quasi-meditations. A beautiful, simple tune played skillfully many times in a row alters your mood and helps you become calmer and more present. Over time, calmness and presence become your primary habit, enhancing your creativity and speeding up your learning of everything, not just the materials in this book.
- Musical archetypes, or compositional snippets that seem primitive but that carry the potential to encompass large territories in music.
- Step-by-step practical explorations of some of the foundational materials of music, including vibration, acoustics, the circle of fifths, the harmonic series, tendency tones, and counting.
- Original compositions, some extremely short and easy to play, others longer and more demanding. My sources of inspiration include Minimalism, Brazilian and Latin American folk and pop, and New Age; and composers such as Béla Bartók, György Ligeti, Conlon Nancarrow, Gustav Mahler, Hermeto Pascoal, Thelonious Monk, and many others. I don't mean that I compose like these great musicians, only that my music may have faint inklings of their styles.
- Entry points to improvisation and composition, including for beginners without compositional experience or knowledge of music theory.

A Fellowship of Learners

I grew up in Brazil, and my mother tongue is Portuguese. I learned English while at university in the United States, and I learned French when I moved to Paris more than three decades ago. In recent years I've been studying Spanish. I spend a lot of time taking lessons, reading novels and essays in Spanish, traveling in Spanish-speaking countries, watching Spanish-language movies without subtitles, listening to a Mariachi radio station, and so on.

Photography and drawing: I'm forever learning about them. Art history: there's so much to learn! In a parallel universe I'd be a visual artist, curating interesting exhibitions in an exquisite museum built by Tadao Ando.

Within the domain of music, my learning has included the usual conservatory subjects such as ear training, theory and analysis, chamber music, and orchestra. I trained primarily as a mainstream cellist playing the canonic repertory. Later on, I learned to improvise and to compose; I learned to sing in a particular style; I learned to play the Native American flute. Now I'm learning to play the guitar.

My main professional activity consists in sharing my learning processes. I'd say I'm a professional learner.

Some years ago I started taking piano lessons, having concluded that my limited pianistic abilities were hampering my overall musical development. My teacher is Alexandre Mion, a wonderful musician who has been my friend, student, and adoptive brother practically since I first arrived in Paris. *Creative Health for Pianists* is partly a result of my conversations with Alexandre Mion, and partly a result of my learning-through-sharing. I've shaped and reshaped my materials thanks to my encounters with pianists of all abilities.

Based on my experience, I see four types of pianists who could benefit from *Creative Health for Pianists*: beginners who are comfortable reading music, skilled musicians who aren't trained pianists and who would like to play the piano better, piano teachers, and accomplished pianists who are curious about a different entry point into the labyrinth of music.

Beginners

On multiple occasions, something like this has happened on my watch: A beginner is sitting at the instrument in fear, incoherence, and self-doubt. "I'm not good at this. This reminds me of my childhood. My mother . . ." I invite the beginner to play two notes, then two more notes: four notes forming a special chord that I describe in chapter 1. "It's not supposed to be this easy. Not for me, anyway." I invite the beginner to transpose the chord up by a second, or down by a second. Stay with the white keys. Keep your hands shaped just so; lift them a little; move them a little to the right, or to the left; play. The first chord now lives in relationship with a second chord. This changes everything. "I don't understand what's happening." This early in the journey, understanding isn't necessary, and it might even hinder you. Actually, understanding doesn't hinder you, but the desperate grabbing for understanding, which comes from fear, does. "Okay." And the beginner strikes two, three chords in succession, eight chords covering an octave—a tune, and rather pretty. "Wait a minute!" The total beginner is now a pianist, composer, improviser, musician, and artist. Still a total beginner, but a musician anyway. The transformation is so marvelous that neither of us can explain it.

Creative Health for Pianists is designed to help you become a different type of beginner.

Each chapter starts simple and ends complex. You'll be able to play the simpler version of most exercises and compositions without too much effort. Challenges are presented one at a time, usually with preparatory steps that make the climb easy. You can learn the book linearly, from the first page to the last. Or you can tackle the easy bits in each chapter before attempting the more complex materials. When chapter 2 starts getting too dizzy-making for you, skip to the opening pages of chapter 3 or 4, for instance.

Creative Health for Pianists is a useful support if you're learning the piano with traditional methods such as the famous *Notebook for Anna Magdalena Bach*, Béla Bartók's equally famous *Mikrokosmos*, or graded selections from the repertory from Mozart to Prokofiev and beyond. Two qualities make *Creative Health for Pianists* a fine complement to these excellent and well-known methods:

1. Explanations, suggestions, metaphors, analogies, and the occasional joke, which on the whole are missing from the literature.
2. The constant offer of space between you and music. This is the physical and psychic space in which you can think, feel, and decide for yourself what you want to do and how you want to do it. The space comes from my explanations and the way I introduce my materials, but also from my compositions themselves.

If your score-reading skills aren't advanced, you can use the book to improve score reading itself, as the materials get more demanding gradually within each chapter and from chapter to chapter. The first two chapters, for instance, take place entirely in the white keys (with a single exception, which is a hair-raising piece in chapter 2).

If you don't read music, you could in principle learn many or most of the book's materials by ear with the help of a sympathetic teacher and the book's video clips. The performance clips listed at the end of the book cover perhaps 70 to 80 percent of the book's compositions, and would help you learn the pieces by ear. Nevertheless, the inability to read music is likely to slow down your progress and diminish your enjoyment of *Creative Health for Pianists*.

Trained Musicians Who Aren't Trained Pianists

Instrumentalists, singers, conductors, and composers have often studied the piano alongside their main areas of musical exploration. Sometimes these musicians become first-class pianists. One example is the late Mstislav Rostropovich, the cellist and conductor who occasionally performed as a pianist, accompanying the singer Galina Vishnevskaya (who was his wife).

Average musicians who aren't trained pianists tend to have gaps and blockages regarding the piano. And these gaps tend to come with harsh judgments: "I can't play the piano, I should be able to do it, I should have learned it years ago. It's too late now. I'm embarrassed about it."

This was my own case. I received basic piano instruction in college, and I had to pass exams that consisted mostly in playing a few scales in major and minor keys. But during those years I was so busy with my doubts and confusions that I never really got the hang of the piano. My friendly and competent teachers were Marianna Khazanova-Salzman and Daphne Spottiswoode in college, and Elizabeth Sawyer Parisot in graduate school. Here's me now, thanking them for their efforts on my behalf back then. "Please accept my apologies for having taken forty years to learn what you were trying to teach me."

Creative Health for Pianists brings together technical materials, musical ideas, and psychological concepts that allow the untrained pianist to put harsh judgments aside, catch up, and become a better pianist quickly. Trained musicians will appreciate the in-depth and practical discussion of the circle of fifths, for instance, or the harmonic series. *Creative Health for Pianists* will keep you company as you further your appreciation of these essential aspects of musical life.

Piano Teachers

My concepts and exercises help you sense the relationship between musical materials and psychophysical responses. Seemingly banal chords or rhythms turn out to be rather energizing. This chord makes your hand want to behave in a comfortable and reassuring way. This rhythm is like a horse that you can ride in pleasure and joy, and the horse does some of the physical work for you if you learn to trust it. Almost despite yourself, you make startling improvements to your playing—startling because the chord or the rhythm or the listening exercise appears too modest, too innocent, too plain to have such an impact.

This is catnip to a piano teacher. Innocent materials that trigger startling improvements? "I need to share this with all my students." Behind the innocent materials lies the paradigm that asks you to reorganize your thinking processes and to redefine piano technique. The paradigm hints at solutions to long-standing problems, the removal of blockages, the possibility of expressive and meaningful playing for pianists of all ages and abilities. It's not a panacea and it's not magical; it takes work to make it work. But *Creative Health for Pianists* offers you a grid of useful tools. Roughly speaking, the book's ten chapters each contain thirty exercises and compositions, for a total of 300 musical concepts of various lengths and depths. And let's say that each exercise can be varied in twenty different ways. This makes for a database of 6,000 exercises, allowing for you to juxtapose exercises in untold combinations, each combination tailored for an individual student.

Accomplished Pianists

If you've played everything from J. S. Bach to John Cage and György Kurtág, happily passing through the mavericks, the experimenters, and the lesser composers from faraway lands, you're ready to look at my materials and find something of merit in them. Video clips 1 and 48, which introduce and conclude the book, highlight performances of a few of my compositions by professional pianists.

A method like *Creative Health for Pianists* needs to explain basic concepts in detail, but nothing stops you from leafing through the book, seeing what's there, ignoring the details, and sight-reading a couple of pieces on a rainy Friday evening when you're alone in the house.

But *Creative Health for Pianists* holds a certain potential that merits discussion. I'd like to describe an illustrative encounter with a professional pianist I'll call Myriam. She takes lessons with me once in a while, with the general idea of becoming more comfortable at the piano. In one eventful lesson, this happened:

1. Myriam played a passage by Beethoven. The topmost layer of her interpretation was self-judgment (and it was negative). Her playing was jagged and hesitant.
2. I asked her to put Beethoven, that triggering pest, aside.
3. From the database I plucked an archetype that approximated the musical essence and physicality of Beethoven's passage.
4. I persuaded Myriam to practice the archetype, which happens not to be a triggering pest. In fact, the archetype is very, very easy to play very, very well.
5. I invited her to play her Beethoven again.
6. Judgment had dissipated, and both Beethoven and Myriam shone.

At the end of the session, Myriam lingered and asked a few hesitant questions, lingered and didn't say much, lingered and fell silent. In my opinion, she had undergone a paradigm shift and "had become someone else," a different type of pianist who embraced new priorities and who played not in pain but in pleasure. Myriam didn't understand how it had happened, and she didn't want to leave the strange place where old hurts and frustrations had dissipated, if only temporarily.

For me, witnessing her silent lingering was like looking at a baby in a maternity ward: Myriam was reborn.

A paradigm shift is consequential. It entails letting go of assumptions and habits that have defined your identity over decades. Letting go is by no means easy. Paradoxically, it's painful to let go of pain.

Preface

It isn't obligatory for you to undergo a paradigm shift. You may be perfectly at home in your way of doing things, and you'd be right in rejecting the paradigm that I advocate in *Creative Health for Pianists*.

But to be a child again, and to discover the piano as if for the first time... wow (figure 0.1).

FIGURE 0.1 Discovery

Acknowledgments

I researched and drafted *Creative Health for Pianists* at various music studios in Paris, where I was invariably welcomed by friendly faces. I'd like to thank the team at Studio Bleu, the team at Studios Campus, and Philippe Basseville at Pianos Beaumarchais. Monsieur Basseville is a remarkably gracious person, and his piano shop down the block from my home in Paris is a haven of beauty.

Charles Harvey helped me create many images in the book, such as the circle of fifths and the piano keyboards in chapter 5.

David Tepfer provided me with invaluable help in creating the pedagogical video clips, which we recorded at his fabulous Atelier de la main d'or. For some of the performance video clips I also had the support of the personnel at the Conservatoire de Musique et de Danse de Trappes, outside Paris. I'd like to thank the director of the Conservatoire, Arnaud Morel; and the technicians who recorded the clips, Bruno Leguédois and Émilien Rannou.

A group of musicians of various stripes put time, thought, and effort into recording performance video and audio clips. It's been wonderful to witness my compositions being brought to life by these devoted friends: Mona Al-Kazemi, Jorge Baeza Stanicic, Jon Breaux, Rosana Civile, Lara Erbès, Renato Figueiredo, Karolina Glab, Helen Kashap, Petra Lipinski, Bonnie Lubinsky, Lorenzo Marasso, Carla Marchesini, Dellal McDonald, Magdalena Portmann, Alison Roper-Lowe, and Viki Roth.

A few people came to my aid regarding the project's passage from the private domain of thoughts and feelings to the public sphere of manuscript review and acceptance. I'd like to thank Polly van der Linde and Mira Sundara Rajan for their handiwork.

Creative Health for Pianists wouldn't exist without the steady assistance of Norman Hirschy at Oxford University Press. I can't thank him enough for his patience and encouragement. And I'd like to thank Suzanne Melamed Ryan, who was there for me in the project's tender early days.

My wife Alexis Niki was my trusty sounding board, witness, and foil. Echoes of our friendship reverberate throughout the book.

Pedro de Alcantara
Paris, May 31, 2022

About the Companion Website

www.oup.com/us/CreativeHealthforPianists

Oxford has created a website to accompany *Creative Health for Pianists*. The site contains a collection of forty-eight video clips illustrating some of the book's materials. Clips available online are indicated in the main text with Oxford's symbol ⊙.

Most clips are short. I wanted the clips to show you only the gist of this or that technique, the better to give you a chance to sort things out for yourself. The concepts and tools in *Creative Health for Pianists* are like toys. The clips are prompts, inviting you to play with the toys. And the book itself is the toys' instruction manual, methodical and detailed.

Separately from these pedagogical clips, I gathered a large collection of performance clips in which friends and colleagues of mine explore my compositions. I didn't want these performances to interfere with your personal discovery of the book's materials, and I've kept them apart from the main text. The performance clips are hosted on my website. Please visit www.pedrodealcantara.com/piano. For more information, refer to the section titled "Resources" at the end of the book.

Video Clips

Introduction
 1. Creative Health for Pianists

1, "Dialogue"
 2. Dialogue
 3. Sonic Clashes and Caresses
 4. The Practice of Counting
 5. Germinating Seed, Variation, Composition

2, "Heartbreak"
 6. Heartbreak
 7. Horizontal and Vertical Journeys
 8. The Power of Intervals
 9. The Skills of Variation

3, "Seesaw"
 10. Seesaw: Horse & Rider
 11. The Hands Sing a Chorale: In Estonia
 12. Sympathetic Resonances: Marrakesh
 13. Bursts of Improvisation

4, "Celeste"
 14. Celeste
 15. Repetitive Practice
 16. The Harmonic Series

17. Hymn to the Pedal
18. Forest Stone
19. Pacific Sunrise
20. Sonic Sculpting

5, "The Circle"
21. The Circle of Fifths
22. The Skills of Transposition

6, "Gesture"
23. The Crawler
24. Crossing Hands
25. Improvising to a Constraint
26. Singing Thumbs
27. Nested Thumbs

7, "Advanced Seesaw"
28. The Party
29. Cloverleaf
30. Aloysia
31. Left Aloysia
32. Seesaw of Heartbreak
33. Odd Man Blues
34. Catch the Breeze

8, "Sonic Play"
35. Intertwining
36. Albers
37. The Albers Sequence
38. Transpositions by Thirds
39. Smooth Transpositions

9, "Horn Call"
40. Canyon
41. Mahleriana
42. Mano Sinistra

10, "Mudra"
43. Mudra
44. Shapeshifter
45. Kaliště
46. Cats & Dogs
47. Venus Rising

Conclusion
48. Unconditional Love

INTRODUCTION

Creative Health for Pianists is built on what we might call *archetypes*: condensed music snippets that magnetize some aspect of music making and piano playing. The snippets are easy to play and suited for a beginner's exploration. The attitude they encourage might be encapsulated like this: "I'm going to play something simple and beautiful, and I'll learn to play it well and reliably. I'll achieve some degree of coherence and comfort. Then I'll see what I can do when I play something more elaborate."

The archetypes are, for the most part, musically ambiguous. For example, "Dialogue" (chapter 1) starts as a minor second—an interval we always consider dissonant. But it soon becomes a four-note chord that is both dissonant and consonant, both happy-making and troubling, both sweet and sad. These musical ambiguities render the archetypes irresistible to your ears and hands. You start playing them, and you become as if addicted, wanting to find out more, more, more. The archetypes open the floodgates of creativity for the willing pianist at any level.

Chapter by chapter I present these archetypes, explain their logic, and propose technical and psychological tools for practicing. Then I spin each archetype out in exercises, variations, and compositions. Throughout the book I suggest prompts for improvisation, as well as improvisational games with step-by-step rules. These allow a beginner pianist to become an improviser and composer from the first lesson onward. And they allow an accomplished pianist to discover or rediscover enriching aspects of the creative process.

Improvising isn't obligatory. *Creative Health for Pianists* has enough exercises and compositions to keep you busy if you're an incurable improphobic, a condition shared by a lot of musicians.

Here's a snapshot of the book, showing a sample archetype per chapter. This snapshot is a sort of Post-It, showing you perhaps one percent of the whole project. Like all snapshots, it's both true and not true. It gives you a glimpse of the book's individuality, but it doesn't reveal its inner depths.

Introduction

1. "Dialogue" shapes the playing hands into a comfortable and reliable structure (example I.1).

EXAMPLE I.1 Dialogue

2. "Heartbreak" deepens your perception of intervals and their power to communicate beauty and meaning (example I.2).

EXAMPLE I.2 Heartbreak

3. "Seesaw" is the practice of up-and-down actions of playing fingers, with an emphasis on rhythmic drive (example I.3).

EXAMPLE I.3 Seesaw

4. "Celeste" is an exploration of sound, resonance, and sympathetic vibration. It invites you to listen closely, and to become aware of the harmonic series (example I.4).

EXAMPLE I.4 Celeste

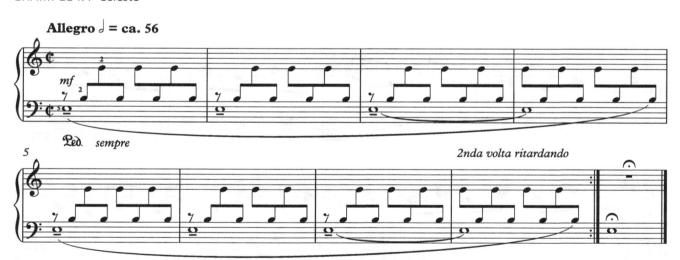

Introduction

5. "The Circle," or the circle of fifths, underpins relationships and hierarches in much of music (example I.5).

EXAMPLE I.5 The Circle

6. "Gesture" highlights the relationship between creative stimulus and physical response. It contains exercises and compositions for each separate hand, for both hands together, and for crossed hands (example I.6).

EXAMPLE I.6 Gesture

7. "Advanced Seesaw" deepens the exploration of the up-and-down movements of fingers as they respond to more complex rhythms (example I.7).

EXAMPLE I.7 Advanced Seesaw

8. "Sonic Play" highlights the collaboration of finger action, rhythm, and sound. The chapter contains multiple entry points to improvisation (example I.8).

EXAMPLE I.8 Sonic Play

Introduction

9. "Horn Call" is an exploration of sound, vibration, and dynamics (example I.9).

EXAMPLE I.9 Horn Call

10. "Mudra" invites you to think differently about your hands at the piano (example I.10).

EXAMPLE I.10 Mudra

To give you some indication of how I develop the archetypes into exercises and compositions, I put together a sampler of what happens in chapter 2 (example I.11). "Heartbreak" starts as a single four-note chord. Arpeggiation; transposition up and down the keyboard; changes in rhythm, tempo, and dynamics; chord voicing; and chromaticism transform "Heartbreak" into a chorale, a waltz, a jazzy piece, and much else besides. *Creative Health for Pianists* invites you to see how embellishment, variation, transposition, improvisation, and composition exist as potentialities in your own musical life.

EXAMPLE I.11 Developing an archetype

Introduction

Note combinations, with their intrinsic beauty, become finger combinations. Each finger combination requires something of you: feel this, pay attention to that; drop, lift, relax, firm up; elbow, forearm, wrist, fingers; joints, skin, flesh, and bones. Certain note combinations and their required gestures have the potential to hurt you, if the notes are awkwardly composed or if you react awkwardly to them. Logically enough, other notes and their gestures have the potential to heal. Music itself might become your osteopath, so to speak, dissipating your awkwardness or your pain. *Creative Health for Pianists* contains multiple concepts to put you on a healing journey.

Two things will help you: an ever-deepening awareness of the basic phenomena of music, and a particular way of thinking about technique.

Play two notes together: C and E♭, a minor third. Not a big deal, right? Except that it *is* a big deal. The interval has a personality, a specific vibration. It's very different from C and E♮ played together, a major third. If you pay attention, intervals like these tell you a lot about consonance and dissonance, subtext and connotation, beauty and meaning. If the interval isn't a big deal, you play it in a certain way; if it's a big deal, you play in a different way. Touch, the transfer of weight from your arm to the keys, timing, dynamics, voicing—nothing is the same. I hope *Creative Health for Pianists* will help you make a big deal of simple but wonderful musical components.

It's often said that healthy technique comes from physical relaxation. I take the view that healthy technique, besides being a creative response to a creative situation, is the result of multiple forces—or *tensions*—brought into balance. You need to plant your feet on the ground, to orient your spine upward, to integrate your shoulders and back, to lift your arms and hands without stiffening your neck, and to drop the hands toward the piano keys with a specific musical goal in mind. All these activities require a sort of mental presence very different from the relaxation of slouching in front of the TV. Music itself is a form of tension. An interval like a minor third (the C and E♭ of our example) has a built-in musical agitation that implies movement and direction. Sound, too, is a force or energy with tension-like properties. Whenever you play something, oscillations travel in space and impact your eardrums. The balanced interaction of physical, mental, musical, technical, and aural forces might give you the impression that you're relaxed. It's an illusion, or rather a paradox: your whole body is engaged, your whole mind is engaged. And yet your ego stays out of the way and you feel as if you're not doing anything, because music does the job for you. This is healthy technique.

 Video Clip 1, "Creative Health for Pianists."

DIALOGUE 1

Compositions
- Simplicity (example 1.10)
- Higher Simplicity (example 1.11)
- Trivium (example 1.12)
- Stroll (example 1.14)
- Promenade (example 1.15)
- Fingers (example 1.16)
- Mysterium (example 1.19)
- Ceremonial (example 1.20)
- Hello Hemiola (example 1.22)
- Seksy Sesky (example 1.23)
- Tally Up (example 1.24)
- Pentagram (example 1.26)
- Three of Eight (example 1.28)
- Brief Eulogy (example 1.31)
- Eulogy (example 1.32)
- Driven (example 1.35)
- Driven Forward (example 1.36)
- Escalator (example 1.38)
- Charanga (example 1.39)
- Jumping Frog (example 1.40)
- Juventud (example 1.41)
- Tranquil (example 1.42)
- Farewell (example 1.43)

Video clips
2. Dialogue
3. Sonic Clashes and Caresses
4. The Practice of Counting
5. Germinating Seed, Variation, Composition

A well-tuned acoustic piano, fully open and in a resonant room, is a joy. But if all you have at your disposal is an electronic keyboard, it'll be good in its own way. The left thumb plays B, the right thumb plays C—the interval of a minor second (example 1.1).

EXAMPLE 1.1 The birth of a technique: anchoring thumbs

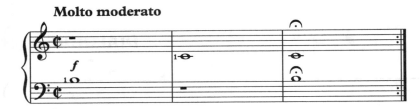

Add two new notes. The left little finger plays E, the right little finger plays G (example 1.2). How fast, how slow, how lyrically, how percussively should you play? You choose. Put these bars on a loop and play them a few dozen times, varying their speed, dynamics, and character.

EXAMPLE 1.2 The birth of a technique: counterweighing pinkies

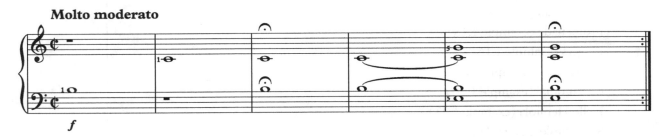

The thumbs anchor the hands, and the pinkies provide a counterweight. The hands are symmetrically organized and placed next to each other. You barely need to do anything to structure the gesture and to feel good doing it.

Vary the order in which you strike the notes (example 1.3). Play them as a melody, as an arpeggio, as a chord. Add the right pedal if you wish.

EXAMPLE 1.3 The beginning of playful exploration

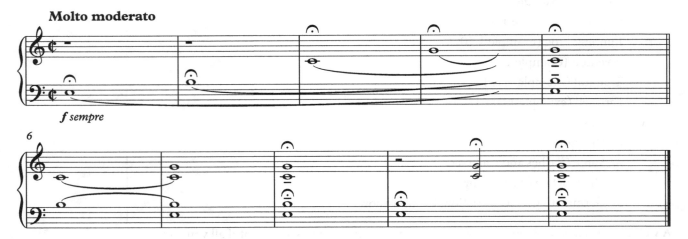

The chord melds two distinct sonorities: an E-minor chord in root position, and a C-major chord in first inversion (example 1.4). Some theorists would call the melded chord a

C-major triad with an added seventh, in first inversion. Major or minor? Caress or clash? Joy or sadness? You could dwell in this chord for a long time without solving its musical ambiguities or your emotional response to these ambiguities.

EXAMPLE 1.4 Musical ambiguity

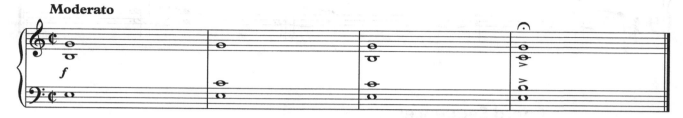

To produce such an interesting musical structure with your bare hands gives you a feeling of power: "I'm a pianist, I'm a musician; I'm the agent of meaningful, deep expression." Strangely, you might also feel that you're not responsible for the gesture or its sonic results: "I'm just putting my thumbs here and my pinkies there. It comes out of its own accord." It's hard to define the "it" that comes out of its own accord: the sound, the music, the emotion, the connection, everything tangled up and interdependent.

"Dialogue" is a conversation between the two hands, between consonance and dissonance, between caresses and clashes. It's nothing but a four-note chord, and yet it deserves to be called an *archetype*—a living idea that can take a thousand different shapes.

Video Clip 2, "Dialogue."

To increase comfort and control, make individual notes louder or softer (example 1.5).

EXAMPLE 1.5 Comfort and control

Use the interplay of dynamics to enhance your perception of the exercise's simple beauty (example 1.6). Activated and magnetized by your attention, the thumbs and little fingers give the hands a special shape, which is relatively firm, while the wrists and arms stay supple. The keyboard becomes a sort of trampoline for the organized hand.

EXAMPLE 1.6 Interplay of dynamics

Chord Sequences

With unchanging fingerings and the two hands close to each other, the chord is easy to transpose up or down a step (example 1.7).

EXAMPLE 1.7 Chord sequences

To the eye, it looks like a double sequence of *parallel fifths*. In fact, you're playing a sequence of *juxtaposed parallel sixths*. For the sake of convenience, they're fingered as if the hands were playing parallel fifths (example 1.8).

EXAMPLE 1.8 Juxtaposed parallel sixths

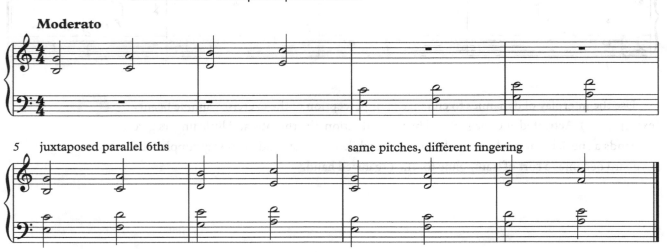

Example 1.9 shows how the same chord can be fingered and voiced to highlight the fifths or the sixths. The exercise compels your thumbs to become intelligent and adaptable.

EXAMPLE 1.9 Intelligent and adaptable thumbs

Using the easier fingering and voicing, let's extend the sequence a little, add rhythmic variety, and calmly go up and down the keyboard until we tweak the sequence at the end of the walk (example 1.10). We've gone from exercise to composition. We'll title our work "Simplicity."

EXAMPLE 1.10 "Simplicity" ©Pedro de Alcantara

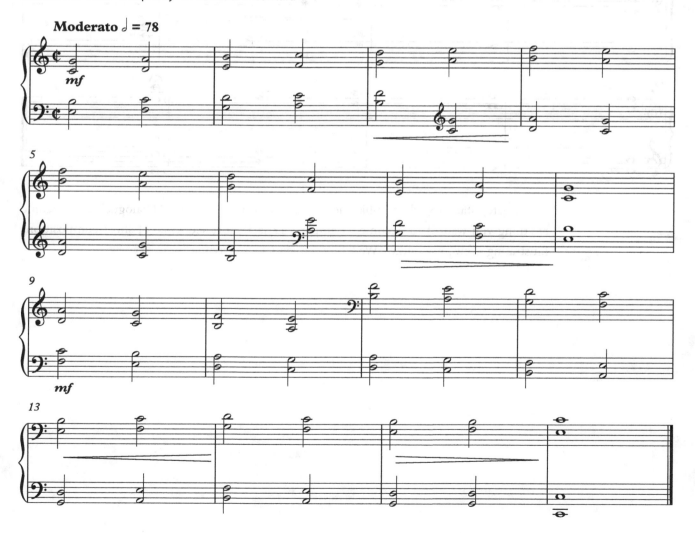

We'll compose something slightly more elaborate, and title it "Higher Simplicity" (example 1.11). After you learn it, play it one octave higher.

EXAMPLE 1.11 "Higher Simplicity" ©Pedro de Alcantara

Legato, staccato; chorale-like, joke-like; caressing, insistent. "Dialogue" can become anything you want it to become. Example 1.12 is a short sequence of short compositions illustrating a few possibilities. We'll title the sequence "Trivium."

EXAMPLE 1.12 "Trivium" ©Pedro de Alcantara

In later chapters we'll practice the skills of transposing phrases and whole compositions to keys both close and distant. For now, we'll limit ourselves to diatonic pieces in C major, which means that we stay within the white keys. When you play sequences of chords in "Dialogue," it's possible to use unchanging fingerings and to keep the shape of your hands the same for every chord. It makes it easy to move up and down the keyboard by intervals bigger than a step (example 1.13).

EXAMPLE 1.13 Intervals bigger than a step

Take the snippet from example 1.13, lengthen it by a few bars, and rewrite its ending. It becomes a composition. We'll call it "Stroll" (example 1.14). Or ignore my composition and create your own with the same general principle. All you need is to keep your hands side-by-side, thumbs and pinkies delineating the interval of a fifth wherever they go.

EXAMPLE 1.14 "Stroll" ©Pedro de Alcantara

Logically, we move on to a composition that alternates movement by step and movement by larger intervals (example 1.15). Its title is "Promenade."

EXAMPLE 1.15 "Promenade" ©Pedro de Alcantara

So far we've used an unvarying fingering, with the hands moving up and down the keyboard with a fixed shape anchored by the thumbs and pinkies. While keeping the basic chords intact, we'll use an alternative fingering that engages the hands differently (example 1.16). I'll say that this is a composition, and I'll title it "Fingers."

EXAMPLE 1.16 "Fingers"

Revisit "Promenade" and overlay it with the new fingering (example 1.17). At first it might feel laborious, but practice and time will help you integrate it. Then choose the fingering that you prefer.

EXAMPLE 1.17 New fingerings

Sonic Textures

Using the right pedal, play example 1.18 with a loud ringing tone, legato sostenuto. Hold the final fermata for a long time and hear the sonic clashes and caresses of the chord's intervals. As the sound decays over the life of the fermata, the clashes and caresses transform themselves in surprising and inexplicable ways.

EXAMPLE 1.18 Clashes and caresses

Video Clip 3, "Sonic Clashes and Caresses."

Put those bars on a loop, and you'll create a simple composition of surprising beauty. Or take its basic idea—a sonic clash and a repetitive structure with lingering chords that allow you to pay attention—and start composing something more elaborate. In example 1.19 I show you a possibility. At the risk of appearing pretentious, I'll title this composition "Mysterium."

EXAMPLE 1.19 "Mysterium" ©Pedro de Alcantara

Change the chords at a stately pace, choosing how many repeats per chord (example 1.20). You can weave dozens of variations on this particular exercise. I'll title my variation "Ceremonial." It goes by slowly enough for you to place the chords, the intervals, and the pedaling. And it goes by slowly enough for you *to hear everything*.

EXAMPLE 1.20 "Ceremonial" ©Pedro de Alcantara

Here we are, engaged in a creative process. It doesn't matter if our compositions and improvisations are simple, or even extremely simple. We know that Johann Sebastian Bach and Wolfgang Amadeus Mozart composed great masterpieces, and we know that when we tinker with "Dialogue" we're being very, very modest from a musical and compositional point of view. Bach and Mozart are giants, and we're children at play. We don't mind it!

Counting

Counting is such a fundamental human activity that we could write a whole encyclopedia about it. The little kid who learns to count from one to ten using her fingers is entering the vast world of mathematics—a world in which she'll dwell 24/7, as it were: singing, dancing, skipping, jumping rope; keeping track of the days of the week, keeping track of how old she is; adding cookies to her lunch box, then subtracting them one by one; learning algebra, then trigonometry and calculus; becoming an architect.

Counting is central to life. Therefore, counting is central to the life of a musician.

In music, counting tasks involve time signatures, relationships of duration among notes, metronome markings, and many other aspects. These mathematical dimensions are intertwined with the linguistic pushes and pulls within music.

A feeling for note groupings improves your ability to count rhythms accurately. Here's an illustrative example: "To be, or not to be." We count six syllables in three groups of two syllables. The first syllable is a preparation, the second a stress: "To BE, | or NOT | to BE." Counting, grouping, and linguistic expression must—*must!*—work together in your musical life.

In *Creative Health for Pianists* we've been counting from page one onward. So far we've dealt with simple rhythmic structures that are repetitive and predictable, using standard time signatures. Now we'll spice things up with a few illustrative examples. The chords of "Dialogue" aren't difficult to play. It means you can concentrate on your counting-and-speaking tasks instead of worrying about notes, fingerings, and chord changes. Generally, we'll start each example with a barebones preparatory pattern, to which we'll add one or more complications. And, yes, if you're a beginner some of these complications will complicate your life. To panic, or not to panic? That is the question.

1. You can subdivide a set of six equal elements into two groups of three, or three groups of two. A *hemiola* is a superposition or juxtaposition of these groupings (example 1.21). "Hello Hemiola" introduces the use of the hemiola with the pattern from "Dialogue" (example 1.22). "Seksy Sesky" develops it (example 1.23).
2. "Tally Up" shows you something straight and something crooked (example 1.24). Look closely and you'll see a hemiola in there, plus some interesting displaced accents. It'd be easy for you to transpose it to other chords from the "Dialogue" deck of cards, and to string a sequence of chords using the building blocks of "Tally Up."
3. "Pentagram" introduces the five-count pattern. I show a preparatory snippet (example 1.25), then the composition itself (example 1.26). Play it fast, play it slow; play it as written, transpose it up or down an octave.
4. "Three of Eight" employs an asymmetrical rhythmic pattern much used in jazz, Latin music, and folk music all over the world, sometimes referred to as "three plus three plus two." Different times signatures are used to display it. Example 1.27 lays out the same pattern under three different time signatures, with a little counting track displayed above it. On the counting track you can see the three-plus-three-plus-two mechanism at work.

Musicians have strong feelings about time signatures. Some really hate the compound signature $<3+3+2>\over 8$, others adore it; some find the time signature $8\over 8$ misleading, others are indifferent. My preference is to use the compound signature whenever I compose something with this pattern, as in "Three of Eight" (example 1.28) and elsewhere in the book. In video clip 4 I show you how to practice the materials of "Three of Eight" by simplifying the composition and adding complications one by one. This allows you to get the hang of <3+3+2/8> before having to deal with relatively fast chord changes.

Video Clip 4, "The Practice of Counting."

EXAMPLE 1.21 The hemiola

EXAMPLE 1.22 "Hello Hemiola" ©Pedro de Alcantara

Creative Health for Pianists

EXAMPLE 1.23 "Seksy Sesky" ©Pedro de Alcantara

EXAMPLE 1.24 "Tally Up" ©Pedro de Alcantara

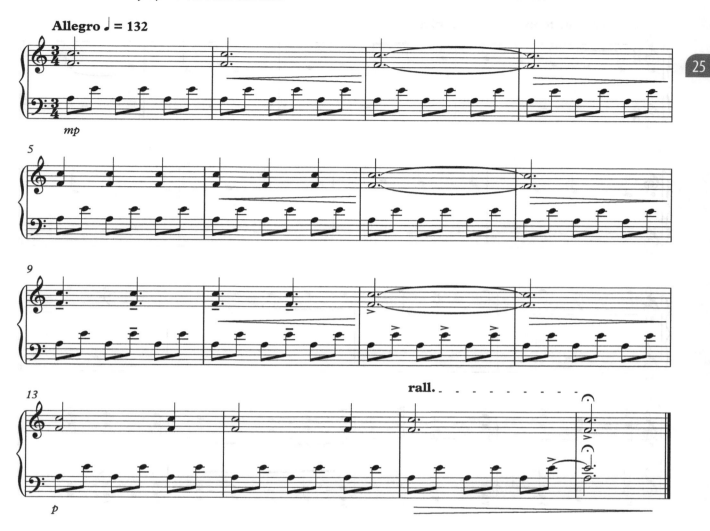

EXAMPLE 1.25 Counting to five

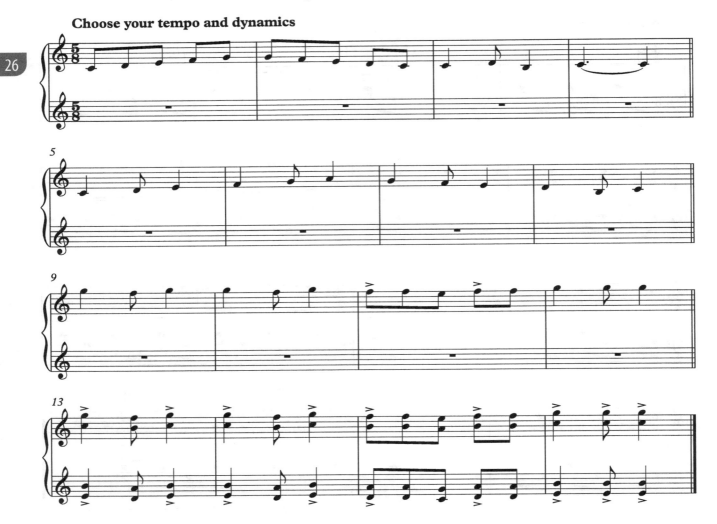

EXAMPLE 1.26 "Pentagram" ©Pedro de Alcantara

EXAMPLE 1.27 Time signatures

EXAMPLE 1.28 "Three of Eight" ©Pedro de Alcantara

From Archetype to Variation, Improvisation, and Composition

We'll engage in an organic creative process that goes like this: germinating seed or archetype; variation and improvisation; composition. The process doesn't require complexity. The germinating seeds, the variations, and the compositions can all be simple. But simplicity isn't obligatory either. Ever-increasing complexity is a worthy goal.

Choose a time signature, a tempo, articulations and dynamics. Play a sequence of chords or arpeggios from "Dialogue," going up and down the keyboard by steps, aiming for some coherence. This is a simple composition.

Tweak the rhythms, change the chord sequence to allow for movement larger than by a step. Allow for the pattern to be broken. This is a more elaborate composition.

Through a series of cumulative transformations, we might get to Scarlatti, then to Beethoven, then to Brahms and beyond. *Creative Health for Pianists* offers only a glimpse of this infinite process, an entry point for your explorations.

Example 1.29 shows a few rhythmic patterns that you can use to vary "Dialogue." It wouldn't be too difficult for you to expand this little database with rhythmic inventions of your own.

Creative Health for Pianists

EXAMPLE 1.29 A database of potentialities

To illustrate the passage from variation to composition, I'll pick one of the rhythmic formulas from my database (example 1.30).

EXAMPLE 1.30 A prompt

The snippet is a suggestion or prompt. It invites you to "play with it," literally and symbolically. Your improvisations can be simple or elaborate, informal or structured, repetitive or varied, irritating or wonderful; it doesn't matter, what matters is to develop the habit of improvising.

I'm sharing two of my responses to the prompt, one short and inconclusive, the other longer and more affirmative: "Brief Eulogy" (example 1.31) and "Eulogy" (example 1.32). Both pieces invite the practice of pedaling. I left much of "Eulogy" without pedaling marks, inviting you to take the initiative.

EXAMPLE 1.31 "Brief Eulogy" ©Pedro de Alcantara

Creative Health for Pianists

EXAMPLE 1.32 "Eulogy" ©Pedro de Alcantara

Let's create another sequence from archetype to variation to composition.

1. In example 1.33 the thumbs play repeated quarter notes. Very easy, right?
2. In example 1.34 the little fingers play half notes, displaced by an eighth-note upbeat. Doable with a little extra practice.
3. In example 1.35 we start moving the pattern by steps, at a predictable pace. If you get the hang of the previous step, it's perfectly doable. I call this composition "Driven."
4. In example 1.36 we spice up the pace of movement and we add an ending that ignores the pattern. I call this composition "Driven Forward." Chords and fingerings remain predictable almost to the very end. The greater difficulty lies in reading the score and figuring out the counting, but the preparatory steps take the sting out of it.

EXAMPLE 1.33 Thumbs

EXAMPLE 1.34 Thumbs and little fingers

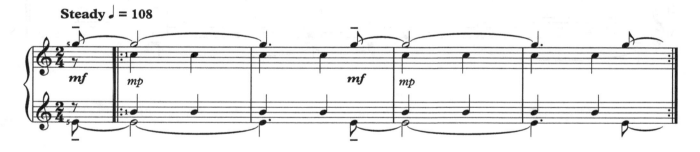

EXAMPLE 1.35 "Driven" ©Pedro de Alcantara

EXAMPLE 1.36 "Driven Forward" ©Pedro de Alcantara

Let's do another step-by-step composition, now with more ambitious goals.

1. We'll start with our archetypal chord, transposed. Then we'll choose a rhythmic pattern, plus tempo, articulation, and dynamics (example 1.37). There's some counting involved, but nothing too worrisome.
2. We'll transpose the chord up or down by a second, sometimes every two bars, sometimes every bar (example 1.38). Essentially, this is an embellished but straightforward scale. Only at the end do we break the pattern with a cadential formula. We'll title this composition "Escalator."
3. We'll add a couple of rhythmic accelerations, and transpose the chords at varied rates—sometimes every two bars, sometimes every bar, sometimes every note (example 1.39). We'll give this composition a title reminiscent of Cuba and Habana: "Charanga."
4. We'll take the left-hand interval and open it up, transposing the lower note down an octave and creating nice leaps for the left hand (example 1.40). I've added a couple of preparatory steps before the leaping starts. We'll call this composition "Jumping Frog."
5. We'll change chords by steps greater than a second, increasing the composition's complexity and difficult of execution (example 1.41). We'll title this new composition "Juventud."

In video clip 5 I show an abbreviated version of the path taken through these compositional variations.

Video Clip 5, "Germinating Seed, Variation, Composition."

Let's imagine two pianists. One is a keen but awkward beginner, the other is a highly trained professional. The beginner might feel threatened by the increased complications. Take it easy, linger on a preparatory step, practice slowly. Remember that the archetypal chords are comfortable to play. Alternate the study of the complications with the study of the simplifications, to coin a concept.

The trained professional might become impatient with these endless repetitive preparatory steps. Skip them, I say! Or show us that you can sight-read each variation to perfection. Or transpose pieces to distant keys. Or add a melody with lyrics of your own, and play and sing at the same time.

EXAMPLE 1.37 Bounce

EXAMPLE 1.38 "Escalator" ©Pedro de Alcantara

EXAMPLE 1.39 "Charanga" ©Pedro de Alcantara

EXAMPLE 1.40 "Jumping Frog" ©Pedro de Alcantara

Creative Health for Pianists

EXAMPLE 1.41 "Juventud" ©Pedro de Alcantara

Any composition you play—your own, those from this book, those from the mainstream repertory—is likely to be the expansion or blossoming of one or more germinating seeds. Seeds can be single notes, scales or scale fragments, rows (as in twelve-tone music), ragas (as in the classical music of India), intervals, chords and chord progressions (as in a passacaglia), motifs, rhythmic patterns, and other elements. Being aware of the relationship between a composition and its generating seeds helps you connect deeply with the pieces you play.

To end the chapter, we'll introduce a new dimension to the pattern, using all the fingers of both hands actively (example 1.42). We'll call this little composition "Tranquil." We'll pair it with a more elaborate version, titled "Farewell" (example 1.43). Played an octave higher, perhaps with softer dynamics, "Farewell" would sound particularly pretty.

EXAMPLE 1.42 "Tranquil" ©Pedro de Alcantara

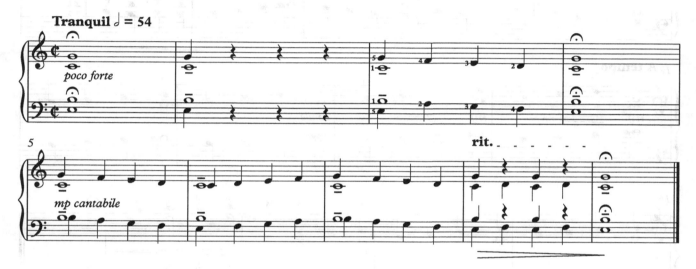

EXAMPLE 1.43 "Farewell" ©Pedro de Alcantara

HEARTBREAK 2

Compositions
- Sustenance (example 2.5)
- Cycle of Heartbreak (example 2.6)
- Muster (example 2.12)
- Little Chorale (example 2.13)
- Chorale (example 2.14)
- Little Waltz (example 2.22)
- Afternoon Waltz (example 2.23)
- Carezza (example 2.24)
- Janus (example 2.29)
- Cradle (examples 2.30 and 2.31)
- I Plead with Thee (example 2.33)
- Ascension (example 2.34)
- Easy Easy (example 2.36)
- Not Too Easy (example 2.37)
- Heartbreak: Triptych (example 2.38)

Video clips
6. Heartbreak
7. Horizontal and Vertical Journeys
8. The Power of Intervals
9. The Skills of Variation

Four notes: simplicity itself, but musically intriguing (example 2.1).

EXAMPLE 2.1 Heartbreak

As with "Dialogue," we start with anchoring thumbs playing a mildly dissonant interval, in this case a major second. When we add the other notes, the certainty that we're handling a

Creative Health for Pianists. Pedro de Alcantara, Oxford University Press. © Oxford University Press 2023.
DOI: 10.1093/oso/9780197600207.003.0003

dissonance is somewhat shaken. Consonance and dissonance have technical and mathematical dimensions, but our ultimate response to them is psychological. These four notes make us happy even though they make us sad. The chord is so fertile that it merits being called it an *archetype*.

Familiarize yourself with the basic gesture, then arpeggiate it in $^6_8$ (example 2.2).

EXAMPLE 2.2 Arpeggiated Heartbreak

How are you going to play the arpeggio? You're the boss: legato or staccato, loud or soft, tenderly or aggressively, to a metronome or freely. Written scores aren't complete in themselves; they become complete through your interpretation. If the composer doesn't add interpretive indications to the score, you add them yourself. Example 2.3 suggests a few things you could do with the arpeggio. The score as written approximates an improvisation. Don't take it too literally.

EXAMPLE 2.3 Articulations and inflections

After getting the hang of the arpeggiated "Heartbreak," transpose it up and down the keyboard (example 2.4). For now, you're limiting yourself to the white keys. The fingerings never change. Choose a tempo to your liking. It's nice to be comfortable and play it at a moderate speed. And it's nice to step out of your comfort zone and play it very fast or very, very slow. It's a bit counterintuitive, but to play super-slow and well is sometimes harder than to play moderately fast and well. I only wrote down two lines of music, but you can extend the exercise to the entire range of the keyboard, back and forth, back and forth.

EXAMPLE 2.4 Moving up and down by a step

For a different effect, sustain each note as you play it (example 2.5). The sustained version looks a little confusing on paper, but it's a delight to play. I like it so much I'll deem it a composition, and I'll title it "Sustenance." I usually shorten the first note played by the right hand, rather than playing all notes equally sustained.

EXAMPLE 2.5 "Sustenance" ©Pedro de Alcantara

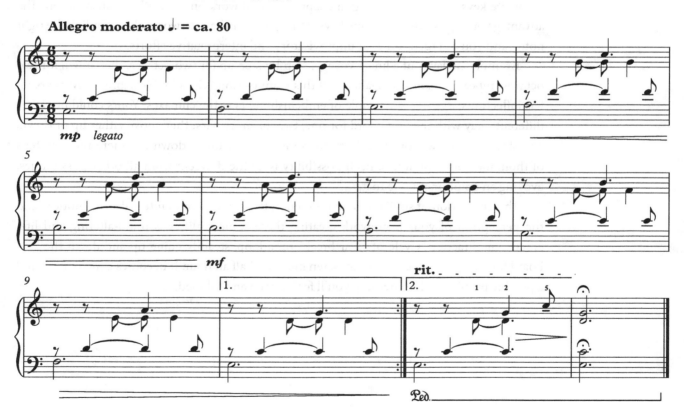

For the sake of visual brevity, some of the time I'll display further versions of "Heartbreak" without the sustained note values. Choose whether you want to sustain, and how much.

What's the piece's tonality? It's ambiguous: C major, with intrusions from A minor; or perhaps there's no separating C major from A minor here. (Maybe it isn't tonal at all, as we'll see later.) To the innocent ear, the sonorities imply a promise: "We're building up chord relationships in ambiguity, but sooner or later we'll resolve it with a straightforward C-major chord in root position, just for you." But the unambiguous resolution never arrives. "Heartbreak" is a broken promise.

Video Clip 6, "Heartbreak."

Interpretation

Being beautiful and easy to play, "Heartbreak" lends itself to the practice of interpretive techniques involving color and time: articulation, inflection, crescendo and diminuendo, accelerando and ritardando.

Your variations and interpretations will sound good, because the song's basic materials are inherently expressive. The song doesn't judge you. Slow is good, fast is good, soft is good, loud is good. You're a good player and interpreter. You're good.

In this game, your compositional efforts are straightforward. You can only do three things: stay where you are, go up by a second, or go down by a second. For now, we don't leave the white keys. Later on (starting in chapter 5) we'll work on the skill of transposition. The advantage of staying with the white keys is that you don't have to worry about finding the right notes, and you can focus on your improvisatory and interpretative efforts.

Example 2.6 lays out a linear voyage: step-by-step up for two octaves, then down for two octaves; repeat it again and again. I call this composition "Cycle of Heartbreak." My version has inflections, dynamics, a couple of embellishments at the climaxes. Yours could be rather different. Stay with the first chord for one, two, or more bars; then move either up or down, and stay for one, two, or more bars; then move either up or down . . . there must be tens of thousands of possibilities. Each possibility is a little different from all other possibilities, evoking an emotion unique to it.

The perception of similarity and difference, the perception of interval and emotion, and the perception of your handiwork creating these sonic realities is mind-altering and life-enhancing. Practice "Cycle of Heartbreak" on a loop, steadily going up and down the keyboard for five minutes, eight minutes, ten minutes, half an hour. It becomes a meditation and a psychic problem solver, because you'll feel relaxed and fulfilled.

EXAMPLE 2.6 "Cycle of Heartbreak" ©Pedro de Alcantara

Creative Health for Pianists

Vertical and Horizontal Journeys

When we first meet "Heartbreak," we see a sequence of jumps and leaps. Although none of the leaps is very high, we still perceive the piece as a vertical exploration: climb, descend, climb, descend (example 2.7).

EXAMPLE 2.7   A vertical journey

It's possible—and easy—to rewrite these arpeggios as four-note chords, and to play the chords in sequence (example 2.8). Our perception of the piece changes considerably.

EXAMPLE 2.8   A horizontal journey

And it's possible—and easy—to rewrite the chords as a chorale in four parts (SATB means "soprano, alto, tenor, bass"). Now we see "Heartbreak" not as a vertical exploration, but as a horizontal voyage, faintly reminiscent of church music (example 2.9).

EXAMPLE 2.9 SATB

Example 2.10 displays the transformation of "Heartbreak" the other way around: from chorale to chords to arpeggios. This emphasizes the horizontal version as the point of departure in the process of transformation.

EXAMPLE 2.10 From horizontal to vertical

You can rewrite just about anything you play to render it more horizontal—or more vertical, if that's what you need. Physically rewriting a piece is useful, but not obligatory. You can simply think and feel your pieces as being more horizontal or more vertical. It takes practice.

Video Clip 7, "Horizontal and Vertical Journeys."

You can use many types of fingerings when playing a sequence of "Heartbreak" chords. Example 2.11 is a database of possibilities, seemingly written by a mad scientist who's addicted to fingering permutations. Play through the example and find out if you too like permutations. The last two lines in the example form a simple composition that makes an emphatic statement: "I want to use *these fingerings* right now! I've had it with all those permutations!"

EXAMPLE 2.11 Fingerings

Let's use the chordal "Heartbreak" and compose something with it. We'll do three versions in increasing degrees of elaboration. For these three pieces, I'll include some fingering suggestions based on the combinations I laid out.

1. The first version is nothing but the pattern itself, moving up or down by a second; we only break the pattern for the last two bars (example 2.12). We'll call our composition "Muster," which is German for *pattern* or *template*. How legato can you play it? Where will you insert breathing pauses for the singers? Is the right pedal going to help you achieve the effects that you're aiming for? It doesn't matter that the composition is extremely simple; it offers you a territory in which to exercise your decision-making skills.
2. The second version keeps the movement up or down by a second, and it adds rhythmic variety (example 2.13). We'll call it "Little Chorale." I added some mad-scientist fingerings, but keep in mind that it's perfectly possible to play the piece with an unchanging fingering for every chord other than the cadential formula: the "Heartbreak" fingering we used at the beginning of the chapter. Tempo, timing, and a little pedaling would allow you to play the piece with a semblance of legato despite the chordal fingering.
3. The third version allows the movement up and down to be occasionally bigger than a step (example 2.14). We'll call it "Chorale." I fingered half of it.

EXAMPLE 2.12 "Muster"

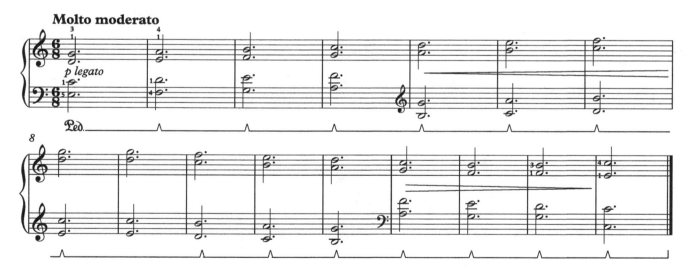

Creative Health for Pianists

EXAMPLE 2.13 "Little Chorale" ©Pedro de Alcantara

EXAMPLE 2.14 "Chorale" ©Pedro de Alcantara

Intervals

We're moved by a sequence of intervals, which we call a melody, which we call a song, which we call art, which we call divine. This happens all the time as we make music or listen to it, but we tend to take the power of intervals for granted.

At the piano, it's tempting to consider intervals as *fingers on keys*, which means getting your fingers into positions and assigning numbers to the fingers, the better to keep track of things. But it's possible to consider intervals as *distances* and *vibrations* instead, each interval having a personality with characteristic emotions. The ascending fourth doesn't trigger the same effect as the descending forth. There's a beauty to the ascending sixth that we can barely explain intellectually. And the beauty of the ascending major sixth is completely different from the beauty of the ascending minor sixth.

"Heartbreak" invites you to shift from thinking of intervals as fingerings, with numbers attached, to thinking of them as sensations and emotions, with meanings attached. You can make

Creative Health for Pianists

the shift in many ways: singing the intervals away from the piano, singing them as you move your hands in space, playing them deliberately at the piano, committing to them, enjoying their power to guide your hands. Isolate the intervals of "Heartbreak," then play each in turn, lingeringly, lovingly (example 2.15). Afterward, retain the feeling of the intervals and play the pattern normally. Create sequences of the main intervals from "Heartbreak" and practice the sequences as if they were meaningful compositions in themselves (example 2.16).

EXAMPLE 2.15 Isolated intervals

Heartbreak

EXAMPLE 2.16 Sequences of intervals

Video Clip 8, "The Power of Intervals."

Note Groupings

When you talk, you naturally create connections and separations in between the words you say. It goes something like this:

When you talk |
you naturally create | connections and separations |
in between the words you say.

Without separations, the text would be incomprehensible:

Whenyoutalkyounaturallycreateconnectionsandseparationsinbetweenthewordsyousay.

With awkward connections and separations, the text would suffer even more:

When you |
talk you nat- |
urally |
create con- |
nections and sep- |
arations in |
between the |
words you |
say.

Groupings make or break the text, and they make or break the speaker. It's the same in music: note groupings make or break the musical text, and they make or break the performer.

In written scores, there are no reliable ways of indicating note groupings in all their complexity. The job is mostly left to the performer—that is, to you. "Heartbreak" allows you to experiment with note groupings. Find out how groupings affect your understanding of the piece and your feeling for it in performance. Example 2.17 is a catalog of possible note groupings within the core of "Heartbreak." The groupings have two, three, or more notes.

EXAMPLE 2.17 Note groupings

In example 2.18 I attempt to show you visually how different groupings affect your playing. The top line shows "Heartbreak" without explicit groupings. There follow two options for interpretive groupings, one symmetrical ("3 + 3"), the other asymmetrical ("4 + 2"). It doesn't look like the same piece, and it won't feel like the same piece when you perform it.

EXAMPLE 2.18 Selecting note groupings

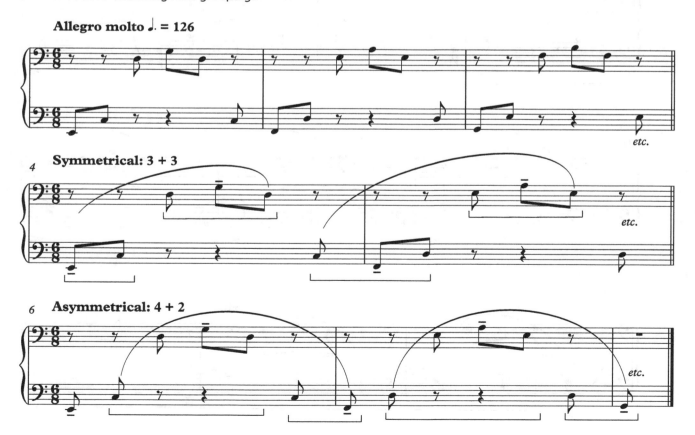

Creative Health for Pianists

In example 2.19 I took the second note-grouping suggestion and laid it over a few bars of "Heartbreak," using articulations and inflection markings. It makes for an awkward visual experience. It's probably more comfortable for you to internalize your note-grouping decisions independently of markings on the score. Like everything else, it takes practice.

EXAMPLE 2.19 Practicing note groupings

Variations, Improvisations, Compositions

Imagine an antechamber adjoining a palace. The antechamber may be impressively appointed, but the palace is infinitely bigger and richer. A musical idea is like an antechamber, adjoining a palace of creative possibilities where variations and transformations dwell. All you need to do is to pass from the antechamber to the palace and discover what's there.

The sounds that you make are the gestures that you make; the beauty of your sounds is the beauty of your gestures; the intricacy of your sounds is the intricacy of your gestures. You vary a musical idea to become "intelligent and beautiful," like the music you play. Example 2.20 suggests a few variations, in increasingly complex rhythms.

Creative Health for Pianists

EXAMPLE 2.20 Intelligent and beautiful variations

Let's take one of these suggested variations ("Tempo di valzer") and use it in our creative process of incremental elaborations.

1. Example 2.21 shows the rhythmic pattern in a simple sequence up and down the keyboard. You can vary the direction and broaden the range of the keyboard over which you travel. What happens, sonically and physically, if you decide to cover the entire length of the keyboard with your back-and-forth, up-and-down waltz?
2. Example 2.22 extends the sequence and breaks the pattern at the end. We'll call this composition "Little Waltz."
3. Example 2.23 further extends the sequence and breaks the pattern in a more elaborate manner. We'll call this composition "Afternoon Waltz."

EXAMPLE 2.21 Tempo di valzer

EXAMPLE 2.22 "Little Waltz" ©Pedro de Alcantara

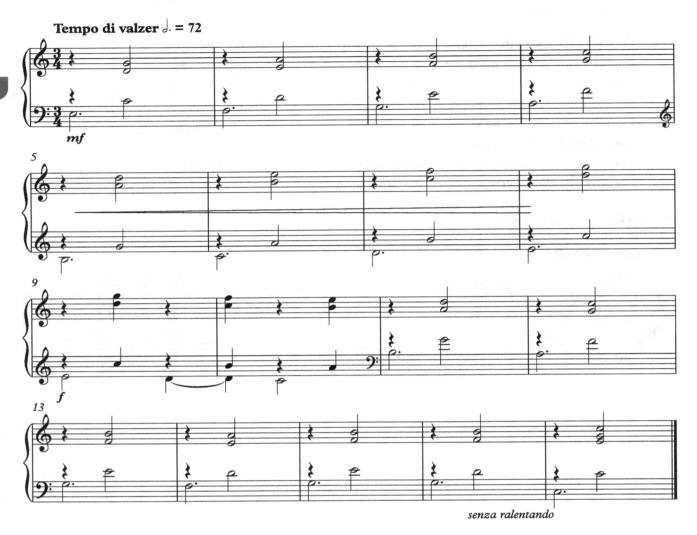

EXAMPLE 2.23 "Afternoon Waltz" ©Pedro de Alcantara

Tonal versus Modal

Example 2.24 shows a new variation: a sustained melody, embellished by a fast arpeggio using the intervals of "Heartbreak." Despite its simplicity, I'm saying it's a composition and am titling it "Carezza."

EXAMPLE 2.24 "Carezza"

The arpeggio's short notes are an interesting challenge. How short, how long? How loud, how soft? How emphatic, how delicate? There are dozens of gradations, each requiring its touch. It's your decision-making, your touch, your gradation, your "Heartbreak."

Change the rhythms: use an alternation of half notes, quarter notes, dotted quarter notes, eighth notes, or anything you want (example 2.25). Go up one or two steps, down two or three. You'll die of happiness and sadness.

EXAMPLE 2.25 Improvising "Carezza"

Play the original "Carezza" as written. Then, play only the scale of half notes without the rolled arpeggios (example 2.26). Never again will a scale of yours be a technical exercise, played indifferently as a duty or obligation. Every scale is, potentially, "Heartbreak."

EXAMPLE 2.26 A heartbreaking scale

The scale is ambiguous. Is it in C major, starting on a G, or is it a Mixolydian scale in G? Imagine you're looking at a photo of an attractive face, but you aren't sure if it's boy's or a girl's; a real person or a computer-generated image; someone alive or someone dead. A scale in C major starting and ending on a G is different from a Mixolydian scale starting and finishing on a G. Pitch for pitch, it's the absolute same scale, but context and connotation will make it tonal or modal. And the emotions of tonality and modality are different, much as a computer-generated image of a dead boy is different from a photo of a girl who's alive, even when the two images look identical. You'll play "Heartbreak" differently if you sense it as tonal or as modal.

What exactly is a Mixolydian mode? Every idea in *Creative Health for Pianists* could be expanded and linked to many other ideas, but this would create a much larger book. As it happens, in chapter 9 I'll briefly explain what the Mixolydian mode is and how it came into existence. But here you must decide: "Do I want to find out more, or am I okay sitting at the piano and playing my exercises and variations without worrying about modes and tonalities?" It's up to you.

The Intelligent Singing Thumbs

Example 2.27 introduces another variation. Looking at it, your eyes risk not seeing an interesting feature: hidden in plain sight, a middle voice sings a pattern (or melody, if you prefer) with driving rhythms.

EXAMPLE 2.27 A hidden melody

The notes of this inner pattern are shared between left and right thumbs. Isolate the pattern and practice it, in pleasure and joy. The variation then becomes easier to play—at any speed, including super-fast (example 2.28).

EXAMPLE 2.28 The intelligent singing thumbs

I spun the variation out as a composition with a complication: the acceleration of the pattern and the alternation of 3/4 and 6/8. I call this composition "Janus" (example 2.29). Since it consists mostly of ascending and descending scales, you could easily keep it going, up and down, deciding when to accelerate the pattern and when to restore it to its starting speed. And after going up and down as many times as you wish, you can bring "Janus" to an end by using the last eight bars of my version or by making up your own ending.

EXAMPLE 2.29 "Janus" ©Pedro de Alcantara

Creative Health for Pianists

The variation in example 2.30 also demands that the thumbs remain intelligent and sensitive, while adding challenges of rhythm and voicing. I'm deeming it a composition and titling it "Cradle." I display it in two versions: with an inconclusive ending, like a question mark (example 2.30); and a more conclusive ending, like a full stop (example 2.31). This is partly to encourage you to make up your own endings, here and in other pieces throughout the book.

EXAMPLE 2.30 "Cradle" ©Pedro de Alcantara

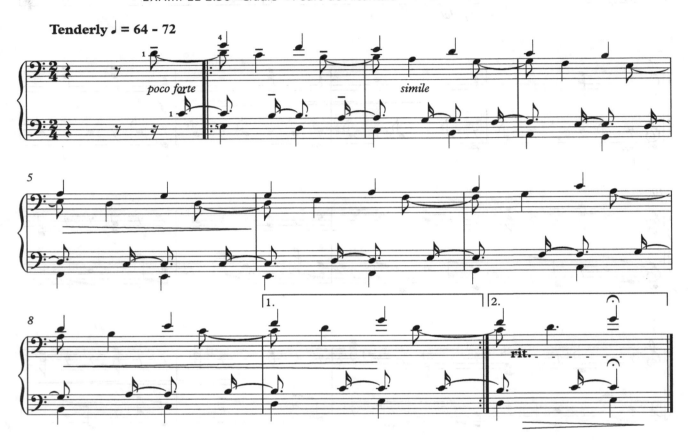

EXAMPLE 2.31 "Cradle, version 2" ©Pedro de Alcantara

On paper, "Cradle" looks complicated. But if you isolate a handful of notes and zoom into their placement and duration, you'll see how the pattern is constructed and who does what, when. Also, the sequence is predictable and symmetrical: the intervals and rhythms of the pattern don't change as you move up and down the keyboard. Get the rhythmic feel for the *pattern*, and the *sequence* becomes easier to play. Example 2.32 shows the same variation, preceded by a few bars clarifying the pattern's rhythmic structure.

Creative Health for Pianists

EXAMPLE 2.32 Pattern and Sequence

Example 2.33 shows an elaboration of this variation. I'm titling it "I Plead with Thee." Video clip 9 gathers brief excerpts from some of the variations we've looked at, including "I Plead with Thee."

▶ Video Clip 9, "The Skills of Variation."

EXAMPLE 2.33 "I Plead with Thee" ©Pedro de Alcantara

Creative Health for Pianists

EXAMPLE 2.33 Continued

The Pattern Stretched beyond Recognition

When we started the chapter, "Heartbreak" was a simple diatonic pattern that we played in predictable symmetrical sequences. There's a lot of merit in knowing how to play something simple and beautiful, and doing it well and reliably. But now we'll abandon simplicity and we'll stretch the pattern to breaking point. I created a composition titled "Ascension" (example 2.34). It starts with the usual pattern, arpeggiated in the way you're now familiar with. But it evolves into a composition with strange chromatics and rhythmic asymmetries, and it's challenging to sight-read, learn, and memorize. If you're a beginner pianist, you may find it unplayable. Consider it a "flash forward" of your future learning, or a peek at a different world. Or learn it slowly, measure by measure. Why not?

Creative Health for Pianists

EXAMPLE 2.34 "Ascension" ©Pedro de Alcantara

EXAMPLE 2.34 Continued

Easy

"Heartbreak" is born of four little notes. What happens if we keep the pitches but change the voicing by transposing the C up one octave and assigning the D to the left hand? We get "Easy" (example 2.35). It's a bit more dissonant than the original "Heartbreak," as it highlights a seventh in the left hand.

EXAMPLE 2.35 Chord voicing

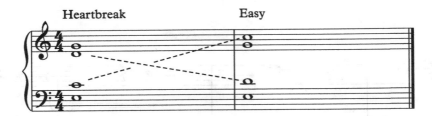

"Easy" is a lovely jazz chord to harmonize a melody with. Using it, I created two versions of a composition. "Easy Easy" is comfortable to play and to count (example 2.36). "Not Too Easy" looks harder on paper, but it's a very similar composition except for the counting part (example 2.37). I've written it as an attempt to capture or to suggest the qualities of swing and rubato—that is, playing with a flexible tempo, not necessarily obeying the metronome. You might be able to play "Not Too Easy" without counting, and relying on feeling instead.

EXAMPLE 2.36 "Easy Easy" ©Pedro de Alcantara

EXAMPLE 2.37 "Not Too Easy" ©Pedro de Alcantara

I end this chapter with a suggestion. Take any two or more short pieces and juxtapose them in performance, as if they belonged together in a compositional sequence. This is a universal principle. A prelude by J. S. Bach followed a fugue by Dmitri Shostakovich, for instance, would make for an interesting juxtaposition. "Easy" followed by "Not Too Easy" would intrigue and entertain some of your listeners.

I became ambitious, and I strung together three pieces from this chapter in a specific order: "Cycle of Heartbreak" (example 2.6), "Ascension" (example 2.34), and "I Plead with Thee" (example 2.33). I composed a quasi-improvisation to bridge the end of "Ascension" to the beginning of "I Plead with Thee." To the resulting juxtaposition I gave the title "Heartbreak: Triptych" (example 2.38). If you find it too difficult to play, limit your juxtaposition to "Cycle of Heartbreak" and "I Plead with Thee," and title it "Heartbreak: Diptych."

Creative Health for Pianists

EXAMPLE 2.38 "Heartbreak: Triptych" ©Pedro de Alcantara

EXAMPLE 2.38 Continued

EXAMPLE 2.38 Continued

EXAMPLE 2.38 Continued

Creative Health for Pianists

EXAMPLE 2.38 Continued

SEESAW 3

Compositions
- Seesaw: Horse & Rider (example 3.2)
- Together Apart (example 3.6)
- In Estonia (example 3.7)
- Arabian Horse (example 3.12)
- Marrakesh (example 3.13)
- Im Nebel Gesehen (example 3.16)
- Im Nebel Schwach Gesehen (example 3.17)

Video Clips
10. Seesaw: Horse & Rider
11. The Hands Sing a Chorale: In Estonia
12. Sympathetic Resonances: Marrakesh
13. Bursts of Improvisation

Our starting point is a five-note scale fragment in E major (example 3.1). These few notes delineate a territory of sonic relationships, gestures, and fingerings. Their combination of white and black keys is friendly to your hands. You'll be more comfortable playing this sequence than the same intervals transposed to B♭ major, for instance.

EXAMPLE 3.1 The comfortable hand

To these notes, we add an archetypal rhythmic structure (example 3.2). I've laid it out in two versions: moderato and lyrical, with multiple fermatas; and fast, driven, and accented. I'm calling this exercise-composition "Horse & Rider."

Creative Health for Pianists. Pedro de Alcantara, Oxford University Press. © Oxford University Press 2023.
DOI: 10.1093/oso/9780197600207.003.0004

Creative Health for Pianists

EXAMPLE 3.2 "Horse & Rider" ©Pedro de Alcantara

It's fun, it feels good, it's challenging at high speed, and it feels good. Yes, I'm repeating myself! Feeling good is all-important!

You propagate what you feel. For this reason, you have a duty to feel good at the piano, to be happy to play, happy to practice, happy to make improvements, happy to learn, happy to share your playing with your listeners. Otherwise, you'll propagate unhappiness and frustration, at a cost to you and to the people around you. It's useful, then, to have a medicine cabinet of feel-good tools.

One such tool is our E-major exercise, since it's clever and pretty. Another is the fermata. You linger on a note, a chord, or a silence because the musical text is enhanced by your lingering. And you linger because you need to and you want to. The fermata allows you to enjoy, relax, sense, feel, think, and decide. "Will I feel good, or will I feel bad? I don't know yet, but I have time to decide. As it turns out, having time for myself makes me feel good."

Your life unfolds in the arena of "allowed, forbidden." When you practice and perform a piece, you don't need to actually linger on notes, chords, and silences. It's enough to feel that you're allowed to linger. The fermata "gives you permission."

Another tool is called *you're the boss*. How fast, how loud, how sustained, how staccato, how resonant, how pedaled? You're the boss. How many repetitions of the same note, pattern, or passage? You're the boss. What are the composer's intentions? You're the composer; the intentions are yours. Someone else (me, for instance) may have offered you a trigger or prompt. This "someone else" may have an agenda, but it doesn't have to affect you. Or it can affect you a bit, without determining your choices and behaviors.

Let's go back to our tune.

Its pattern is logical and predictable once you understand it. Play it slowly a few dozen times, or a few hundred times, and your brain will thank you. Highlight the joinery between bars, and your brain will thank you more warmly still. Joinery helps clarify the structure of a melody, a passage, or a whole movement (example 3.3).

EXAMPLE 3.3 Joinery

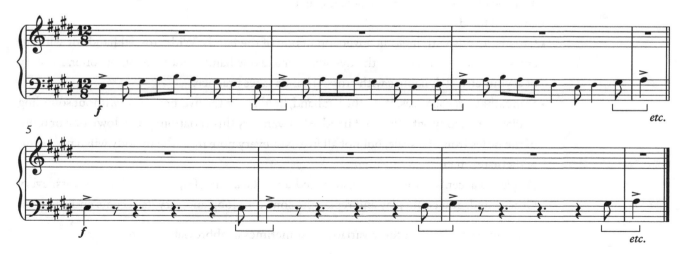

Our exercise-composition requires you to perform the five-note snippet in five different rhythmic configurations (example 3.4). Each note on the pattern takes turns being an upbeat, a downbeat, or a release following a downbeat. Over time, your fingers become able to take on different rhythmic and linguistic responsibilities.

EXAMPLE 3.4 Rhythmic configurations

This is the intricate, structural part of the exercise. Then there's the fun part—the hopping dance, the wit of the tune and the wit of your fingers playing the tune and telling the tune's jokes, to coin an expression. Rhythm, tonality, hand shape, a meaningful musical text, the keyboard's springiness, and your own creativity are working together. We'll call it the *seesaw principle*, in which the up-and-down motions of your fingers are integrated and inseparable from all these other dimensions.

 Video Clip 10, "Seesaw: Horse & Rider."

Variations and Transpositions

How many variations of this exercise-composition can you practice? As many as your imagination allows. Here's a partial list:

- Left hand alone; right hand alone; both hands together.
- Melodic inversion for one of the hands.
- Transposition by one or more octaves, up or down.
- Crossed hands.
- Crossed hands with melodic inversion in one of the hands. With crossed hands or without crossed hands, you can vary the dynamics: make one hand louder, the other softer. Mastery of asymmetrical dynamics with crossed hands takes practice.
- Sympathetic resonances. With the left hand, hold down the five-note scale without sounding it. Play the melody with the right hand. Afterward, try this variation: press down one or more of the notes from the scale, but not all five. Not every note from the melody will have a sympathetic resonator underneath it.
- Displaced accents—for instance, accented upbeats; a mix of upbeats and downbeats; every G♯ accented. You could play and replay the song on a loop and vary its accents endlessly.

Example 3.5 lays out these variations, sometimes in abbreviated form.

EXAMPLE 3.5 Seesaw variations

EXAMPLE 3.5 Continued

Octave transposition

Crossed hands

Crossed hands with melodic inversion

Sympathetic resonances

(hold the keys down without sounding them)

Displaced accents

Example 3.6 introduces a novelty: the right hand starts a tenth above the left hand. It brings asymmetry to the exercise, teasing your brain, ears, and fingers. I call this version "Together Apart."

EXAMPLE 3.6 "Together Apart" ©Pedro de Alcantara

In the variation with melodic inversion, sustain every note played by the thumbs (example 3.7). This creates a texture in four voices, sounding like a folk tune sung by a choir. I call this version "In Estonia," partly because of that country's choral tradition, and partly because some Estonian friends offered me support and hospitality. Slow and lyrical is good—peppy is good too. The song will be prettier if you strike the thumb notes a bit more loudly than all the others. Optional fermatas on some of the downbeats allow the choir to breathe.

Video Clip 11, "The Hands Sing a Chorale: In Estonia."

Creative Health for Pianists

EXAMPLE 3.7 "In Estonia" ©Pedro de Alcantara

When we account for the sustaining thumbs in the score, the song seems complicated to the eyes. And yet it's the same simple song as before, with just a small change. You'll find it easier to understand if you visualize the song in four voices, with each thumb singing and sustaining one of the voices (example 3.8).

EXAMPLE 3.8 Four voices

The Bounce

To be a pianist is to develop the art of the bounce. This means many things.

The rhythms of your musical materials contain their own bounce. Proof of it is that we can talk about a galloping rhythm, a hopping rhythm, a skipping rhythm. Your playing, then, is a response to the bouncy qualities in the music itself.

The mechanism of an acoustic piano is a system of springs, weights, and counterweights. A piano key feels similar to a trampoline. When you press a key down, it's primed to go back up elastically without your having to do anything about it. The keyboard embodies the bounce, with an up-and-down quality permanently at your disposal.

Your body, too, is a system of springs, weights, and counterweights. But when it comes to your own self, it's useful to make a distinction between "doing" the bounce and "allowing" it.

Posture and attitude are essential.

A little child learning to walk must orient her head and neck in space, otherwise she won't find the overall balance that allows her to walk without falling. A tightrope artist also poises her head and neck, thanks to which she has a better reading of the elastic surface upon which she's walking, and a better overall control of body, mind, and gesture. If she misuses her head and neck, she risks an accident, injury, or even death.

Sit at the piano, upright and relatively still. Place your fingers on the keyboard and play our exercise-compositions. The bounce doesn't have to be in your head and neck. You're better off if the bounce is in the music, in the piano, and in your fingers. Suppose you play a swinging version of the tune, full of happiness and joy, marked by strong accents. Even then, remaining upright and relatively still gives you more control of your playing than moving about and shaking your head in time with the tune. Great pianists who embody this principle (which we might also call the *not-moving-too-much* principle) include Artur Rubinstein, Vladimir Horowitz, Arturo Benedetti Michelangeli, Art Tatum, George Shearing, George Gershwin, Magda Tagliaferro, Van Cliburn, Heinrich Neuhaus, Sergei Prokofiev, and Wilhelm Kempff, among many others. YouTube has a vast number of video clips featuring these pianists.

The feeling is that you aren't doing anything and the bounce is "doing itself." Psychologically, it can be "unbelievable" or "incredible," which means that you literally can't believe it. To find the bounce-that-does-itself is easy, but to integrate it and to "believe it" requires a lot of practice (figures 3.1 and 3.2).

FIGURE 3.1 Bouncing

FIGURE 3.2 Bouncing, too

Tendency Tones

We'll take our original E-major scale segment and replace the F♯ with an F♮. This creates the beginning of a scale used everywhere in the world—in India, Iran, and Egypt, among other places; and in Hebrew prayers, klezmer, and flamenco, among other types of music (example 3.9). This beloved scale is called by different names depending on theoretical preference and cultural context. We'll call it the *augmented-second scale,* on account of the interval between F♮ and G♯.

EXAMPLE 3.9 The augmented-second scale

A tendency tone is a note that, to our ears, seems to require movement and resolution. The note "wants to go somewhere specific." In truth, the note itself doesn't have wants and needs. As players and listeners, however, we feel so strongly about melodic and harmonic coherence, consonance, and dissonance that we project our wants on the note. It's a marvelous psychoacoustic phenomenon.

In a short span of five notes, the scale fragment contains an unusual and very expressive augmented second, flanked by tendency tones on both sides (example 3.10). Simple as this may seem, its effect is remarkable.

EXAMPLE 3.10 Tendency tones

Play the fragment over an unchanging drone, and you'll feel the power of tendency tones, particularly in the descending scale: the A really, really wants to resolve to the G♯, and the F really, really wants to resolve to the E (example 3.11). And this musical urgency compels your fingers to move in space and produce the notes in question.

EXAMPLE 3.11 Tendency tones against a drone

Using this fragment, revisit the seesaw variations that you've practiced already. I've laid out a basic version for two hands, which I'm calling it "Arabian Horse" (example 3.12). Watch out for the special key signature, which signals that the G is sharp and all other notes are natural. And pay attention to the special ending that breaks the pattern and spices up the song's end.

EXAMPLE 3.12 "Arabian Horse" ©Pedro de Alcantara

Creative Health for Pianists

In example 3.13 we revisit the version where we employ the sympathetic resonances of notes held but not sounded. Here I call it "Marrakesh."

▶ Video Clip 12, "Sympathetic Resonances: Marrakesh."

EXAMPLE 3.13 "Marrakesh" ©Pedro de Alcantara

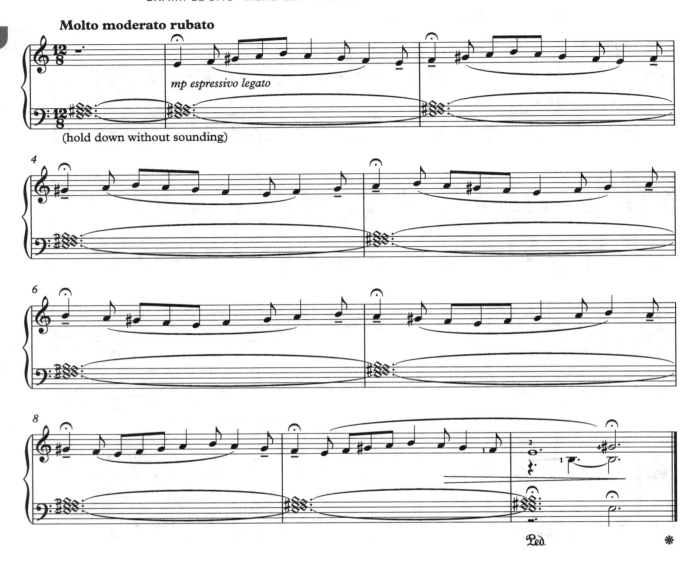

"Marrakesh" is an orderly composition on a predictable pattern. Practicing or performing it, insert bursts of improvisation inspired by the pattern. The fermatas on the downbeats of "Marrakesh" welcome you into this world of improvisation and creativity.

Video Clip 13, "Bursts of Improvisation."

Seesaw Challenges

To optimize the seesaw principle, we've been combining two musical elements: five notes that are easy on the hands, and a driving rhythm in $\frac{12}{8}$. The rhythm plays the role of a horse. Ride it, and you'll find it easier to navigate intervals and fingerings. We'll leave the comfort zone thus far provided by E major and by the augmented-second scale, but we'll keep riding the trusty $\frac{12}{8}$ horse.

Here's a partial list of intervallic possibilities, briefly illustrated in example 3.14.

- All major and minor keys.
- Whole-tone scale.
- Pentatonic scale, starting on any given note.
- Arpeggiated chords: dominant 7th, diminished 7th, and any other chord, transposed to any and all keys.

If you're unfamiliar with modes, tonalities, scales, chords, and their vocabulary, the example gives you enough information regarding these patterns for you not to worry too much about the vocabulary. The score actually shows you what the pentatonic scale is, or an arpeggiated dominant-7th chord.

Creative Health for Pianists

EXAMPLE 3.14 Seesaw challenges

Now I propose an exercise that is both musical and conceptual. It employs an arpeggiated chord similar to those in example 3.14. I chose a B♭ minor chord that starts in second inversion, with an added note that we might call *the leading tone to the dominant*. (And, no, you don't have to worry about the vocabulary.) First, I show the exercise in its basic form: a couple of bars outlining the chord and the rhythmic pattern, ending with the *etc.* mark implying that it's up to you to spin the pattern out to its logical conclusion (example 3.15). Then I show the exercise as a written-out composition with tempo markings, dynamics, articulations, a new fingering for the right hand, a tweak at the end of the pattern, and a Schumannesque title. "Im Nebel Gesehen" means "Seen in the Fog" in German (example 3.16).

The basic version looks like a fast-and-furious finger exercise with the potential to hurt your hands. The written-out composition provides a road map to a mysterious journey of exploration and healing. In the basic version, finger and hand stretches are a physical response to a technical challenge. In the written-out composition, the stretches are a creative response to a creative challenge. Simplifying it, a musical stretch isn't the same thing as a physical stretch. Your fingers can "twist and turn, crash and burn," or they can "think and feel, talk and sing." Plus, you may have noticed that in the written-out composition I changed the fingering in the right hand, abandoning the 1-2-3-4-5 pattern we've been practicing. "Pattern abandonment" is a fine skill to develop. Disobeying someone else's fingering preferences is useful too.

A bar of music, a score, a paragraph in a book, two words on a Post-It: this is information. A sensation, a thought, an emotion, an action: this is how you interpret the information. Ultimately, musical meaningfulness comes not from the information but from your interpretation of it; not from the score, but from you.

EXAMPLE 3.15   A diabolical finger exercise

EXAMPLE 3.16 "Im Nebel Gesehen" ©Pedro de Alcantara

This piece has a lot of flats in its key signature. Suppose it discourages you from learning it. Let's transpose it down a minor second, to the key of A minor (example 3.17). You might find it easier to sight-read, although it's essentially the same piece. We'll be pretentious again and give it a slightly different title: "Im Nebel Schwach Gesehen," which is German for "Seen Faintly in the Fog." The version with a lot of flats is actually easier to play, though it might be harder to sight-read. Combinations of white and black keys are more friendly to the pianist's hands than a surfeit of white keys.

Over time in your pianistic explorations, you'll make friends with sharps, flats, double sharps, and double flats. And you'll also make friends with the art of transposition, which we study in chapter 5.

EXAMPLE 3.17 "Im Nebel Schwach Gesehen" ©Pedro de Alcantara

CELESTE 4

Compositions
- Celeste (example 4.1)
- Celeste: Theme and Variations (example 4.6)
- Axis Mundi (example 4.13)
- Distribuzione (example 4.16)
- Hymn to the Pedal (example 4.17)
- Forest Stone (example 4.19)
- Grace (example 4.20)
- Pacific Sunrise (example 4.22)
- Celestial: In Memoriam ABM (example 4.23)

Video Clips
14. Celeste
15. Repetitive Practice
16. The Harmonic Series
17. Hymn to the Pedal
18. Forest Stone
19. Pacific Sunrise
20. Sonic Sculpting

Many things characterize sound at the piano. The subject is vast, but "Celeste" provides a useful entry point: an archetypal exercise-composition that invites your ears to receive a wealth of information, and that allows you to develop fine gradations of gestures and sounds (example 4.1). The archetype is titled in reference not to a woman's name, but to heavenly matters.

Creative Health for Pianists. Pedro de Alcantara, Oxford University Press. © Oxford University Press 2023.
DOI: 10.1093/oso/9780197600207.003.0005

EXAMPLE 4.1 "Celeste"

Video Clip 14, "Celeste."

Let's rewrite "Celeste" in three voices (example 4.2). Imagine it as a string trio, for instance: violin, viola, and cello. Or three woodwinds: flute, oboe, and clarinet. The main thing is to sense the sonic possibilities of a composition that at first appears excessively simple.

EXAMPLE 4.2 Multiple voices

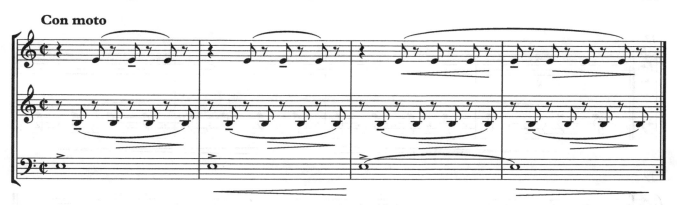

Practice the three voices of "Celeste" independently, varying their dynamics and inflections (example 4.3).

EXAMPLE 4.3 Practicing separate voices

In the normal pianistic version of "Celeste," we can group notes in a variety of ways. Example 4.4 illustrates two main choices.

EXAMPLE 4.4 Note groupings for "Celeste"

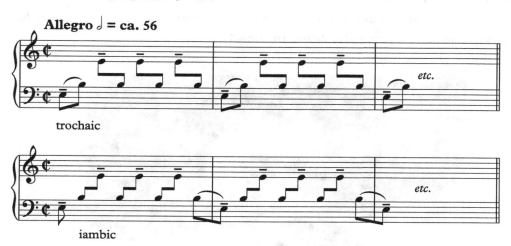

In the top version, every two notes form a group of "stress, release." The first note is a little stronger, louder, or more affirmative than the second one. In the bottom version, the initial note stands alone; afterward, every two notes form a group of "preparation, stress," in which the first note is an upbeat to the second one. To put it differently, you can phrase "Celeste" with or without upbeats. And you can mix and match, creating asymmetry and ambiguity.

Borrowing the vocabulary of poetics, we'll call the combination of "stress, release" a *trochaic foot*, and the combination of "preparation, stress" an *iambic foot*. In this context, a *foot* means a unit that may have one, two, or more syllables (in poetry) or notes (in music).

Trochaic: "SAL-mon | HAD-dock | TU-na | FLOUN-der."
Iambic: "To BE, | or NOT | to BE."

The trochaic and iambic versions of "Celeste" are very different. It's simply impossible to go from one version to the other without changing your thinking and your touch in some way. Music notation doesn't have reliable and unequivocal ways of indicating the composer's preferences when it comes to note groupings. You must do the interpretive work yourself—which is a good thing.

Spinning Your Sounds

A simple composition like "Celeste" serves as a laboratory. Since it's easy to play, you don't have to worry about hitting the right notes. Instead, you can deepen your awareness of other aspects of piano playing. Here I propose a meditation on sound.

When you open a jar with a tight lid, you can scrunch yourself with all your might and force the lid to move; or you can organize your body from head to toe, hold the lid and the jar with a firm but sensitive touch, sense how the thread of the lid meets the thread of the jar, and slowly increase the torque (or rotational power) that you apply to the lid until it obeys your touch and moves along the thread.

Brute force sometimes produces the needed result, but it tends to be costly to the person who deploys it and to the object that receives it. And sometimes it fails altogether. Intelligent sensitivity is more cost-effective, but it robs you of the pleasures of struggling—which, for some people, can be satisfying and addictive (figure 4.1).

FIGURE 4.1 Struggle

Much as you can find the thread in a lid and open it, you can find the sweet spot at the piano and make it ring. You'll feel as if you're spinning your sounds and causing them to circulate and grow inside the piano.

Your general orientation in space is partly responsible for your sound palette. Place yourself in an exaggeratedly awkward posture, sitting too far from the keyboard and bending yourself like a hammy actor trying to "do" a hunchback. Then play the piano. Now sit tall at the piano, with your back wide open and your shoulders relaxed. Play again, and—well, you won't sound the same way. You could decide that you prefer the sounds of sitting scrunched at the piano; that's up to you. The important thing is that different postures create different sounds. Being so easy to play, "Celeste" allows you to try every posture available to your imagination.

Figure 4.2 shows spatial gradations with an interplay of thick and thin lines, forming a nuanced decrescendo from black to white or a crescendo from white to black. Your job is to control all your musical gradations just as thoroughly. "Celeste" and its variations invite exploration. Go from *ppp* to *fff* with a hundred steps between them. Go from adagio molto to prestissimo with a hundred steps between them. Make this note stand out, then make this other note stand out.

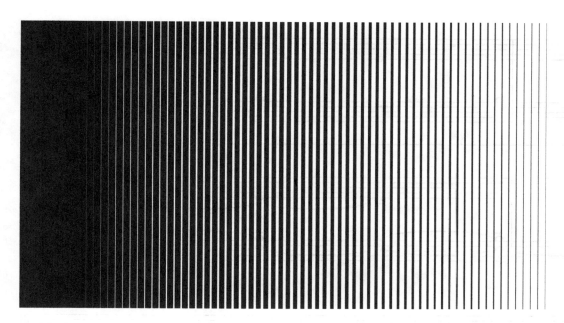

FIGURE 4.2 Gradations

Play "Celeste" on a loop. While varying its dynamics and note groupings, test every possible type of finger action at your disposal. Domed hands, flat hands; high wrists, low wrists; soft fingers, firm fingers . . . the list goes on. Test the point along the piano key where your finger touches it and presses it down. Can you remember to sit tall and relaxed, perhaps without looking at your hands, as you test a hundred finger actions and bodily positions in untold combinations? "Celeste" is a friendly and forgiving framework in which to integrate gesture and sound.

Example 4.5 lays out a few ways in which you can spin the sonic materials of "Celeste." Pedaling, voicing, timing, dynamics, inflections, finger action, intentionality: for the dedicated explorer, the possibilities are huge—even in a minuscule piece like ours.

Creative Health for Pianists

EXAMPLE 4.5 Sonic materials

The Practice and Performance of Variations

Taking "Celeste" as a starting point, I laid out a series of variations in sequence, which you can learn and perform as an actual composition (example 4.6). Its title is simple enough: "Celeste: Theme and Variations."

There are only two pitches: E and B, combined in fourths, fifths, and octaves. There's no melody to speak of. The composer employs no counterpoint, no harmony, no chromaticism, no modulation. Nothing! And yet, the theme and variations are the embodiment of consonance, resonance, and sympathetic vibrations. Precisely because so little seems to be happening, you have the time to hear *everything* that is happening (figure 4.3).

FIGURE 4.3 Oscillations

One of your choices is to follow the exact series of variations as I wrote them down. Another is to play a single variation, perhaps on a repeating loop that lasts forever. Another is to embellish one or more variations with your own ideas. Yet another is to compose and perform your own set of variations. A few of my variations are easy to play; others present counting challenges. To play them, or not to play them? You're the boss.

Should you subject a paying audience to this meager composition in which nothing happens? First, it isn't true that nothing happens. Second, you won't know how listeners will react to any one composition until you perform it. Musical tastes are wide-ranging and subjective. Third, your performance can be terrible or wonderful in itself, quite apart from the pieces you play. A terrible performance of a Beethoven masterpiece can be unbearable. A wonderful performance of a single note repeated endlessly can be unforgettable. Imagine a skillful performance of a subtle composition full of vibrations, using a well-tuned concert grand in a comfortable hall packed with curious and open-minded listeners. Perform each variation multiple times—ten, fifteen times or more, looping the repeats endlessly, with colorful phrasing, dynamics, and voicings. The theme and variations would last an entire concert. In video clip 15 I spin one of the variations on a repeating loop.

▶ Video Clip 15, "Repetitive Practice."

EXAMPLE 4.6 "Celeste: Theme and Variations" ©Pedro de Alcantara

Creative Health for Pianists

EXAMPLE 4.6 Continued

EXAMPLE 4.6 Continued

Creative Health for Pianists

EXAMPLE 4.6 Continued

The Harmonic Series

Play a single note on the piano. It doesn't matter which one, but for the sake of discussion we'll choose the low C. What appears to be a single note is a chord in disguise. At the same time that you sound the low C, you trigger oscillations and vibrations for a huge number of other notes that together form a complex chord. Depending on context, these higher vibrations are called *partials*, *overtones*, or *harmonics*. To keep theoretical explanations to a minimum, we'll call them *harmonics* throughout the chapter.

Example 4.7 shows the low C living the life of a single note, then living the life of a chord in disguise, in which the diamond-headed note represent harmonics. Things in actual piano playing don't happen literally as I depict in the example, which is only a visual approximation of a sonic phenomenon.

EXAMPLE 4.7 A chord in disguise

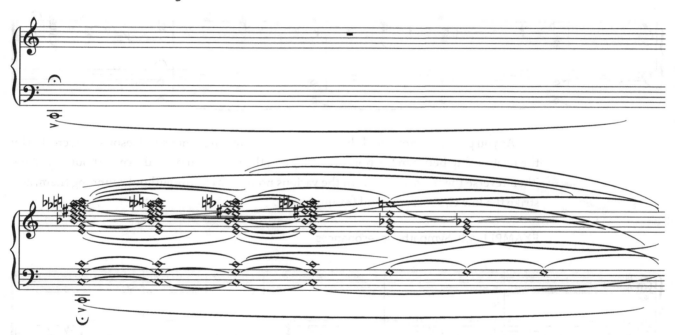

You detect harmonics intuitively. A sound may strike you as beautiful or ugly, muffled or brilliant, trumpet-y or flute-y. Behind these subjective sensations are the harmonics of the sounds you hear: a trumpet-y sound has different harmonics from a flute-y sound. Your job is to become alert to harmonics, to enjoy and cherish their mysterious magic, and to integrate them into how you listen to music and how you make music.

Heightened awareness of harmonics gives you a heightened appreciation of sound itself. Richness of harmonics is the most important element in a beautiful and powerful sound, and you can maximize your harmonics through gesture and timing. Harmonics can become a sort of lifestyle, so to speak, requiring commitment, awareness, and control.

You'll need an acoustic piano to explore and master harmonics. Electronic keyboards can only hint at the phenomenon. Perform example 4.8 on an acoustic piano, without using the right pedal. Diamond-headed notes are meant to be pressed down without sounding.

EXAMPLE 4.8 Hearing harmonics

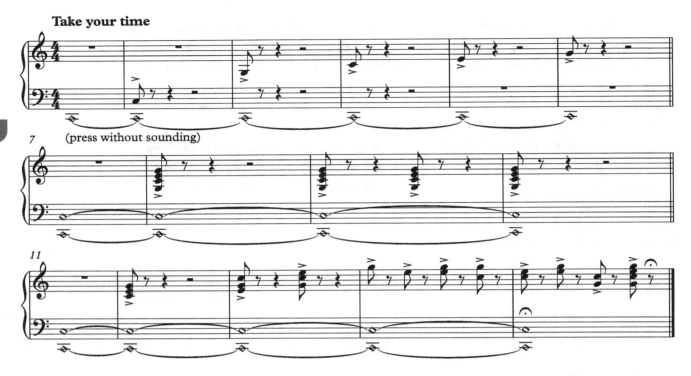

As you play these notes and chords, you'll hear lingering echoes and resonances, created by the relationship between the notes you play and the notes you press down without sounding. Then reverse the roles: press down the various notes and chords without sounding them, and strike the low C, short and loud (example 4.9).

EXAMPLE 4.9 Sympathetic resonances

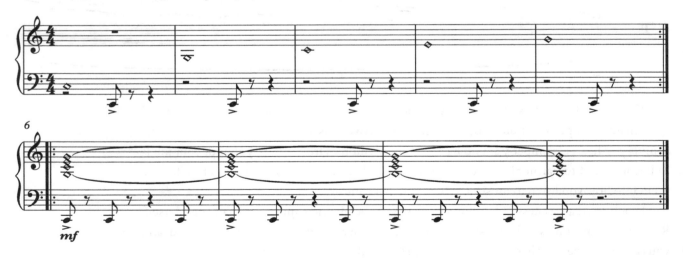

Instead of notes or chords, you can also silently hold a cluster. Lean your left arm across the lower half of the keyboard and press down as many keys as you can, including black keys. With your right hand, play notes, chords, melodies. You'll hear the most beautiful sonic effects.

Then, reverse the role of the hands: push down a right-hand silent cluster and play notes with the left hand.

After these exercises, or in alternation with them, play the low C by itself, in the normal way. You might now hear, faintly or clearly, a chord rich in vibrations. This is true of all notes you play at the piano. And when you play multiple notes at the same time in passages and pieces, the effect is multiplied in amazing ways.

We'll call each note you play at the piano a *fundamental*. Every fundamental sounds its own harmonics, in an infinite series of intervals with ever-higher pitches from the fundamental upward. Mathematics explains the intervallic patterns between a fundamental and its harmonics, but for the sake of brevity we'll leave it out of our discussion. And we'll leave infinity out, too. We'll only study the first sixteen harmonics of a given fundamental.

Sit at the piano and play through the exercise in example 4.10. I suggest that you learn to play the sequence reliably and by heart. The rhythms and fermatas aren't obligatory, but they help you organize and retain the information.

Video Clip 16, "The Harmonic Series."

Creative Health for Pianists

EXAMPLE 4.10 The first 16 harmonics

Several harmonics are difficult or impossible to write down using conventional music notation, because their true pitch doesn't actually correspond to the notes we play at the piano. This is why I propose two versions for some of the harmonics, as in bars 10 and 14 of example 4.10. The second version approximates the true pitch of the harmonics, which is "in between" two normal piano notes.

The last line of the exercise is a sort of memory helper, with a simplified barebones version of the first sixteen harmonics. It's like a police sketch of a suspect. You might recognize the suspect while understanding that there are big differences between the sketch and the actual person it depicts.

We'll take the police-sketch version of the first sixteen harmonics, with its tuning approximations, and pile all the harmonics on top of the fundamental (example 4.11). It more or less illustrates what happens when we strike a low C at the piano. You might recognize this pile of harmonics from the beginning of our discussion, when I wanted to show you the difference between a single note and a chord in disguise.

EXAMPLE 4.11 A fundamental and its harmonics

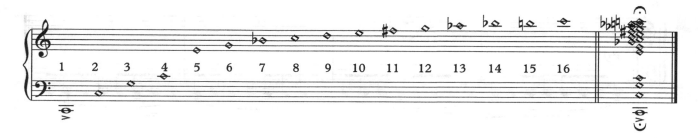

Play a repeated note using the right pedal (example 4.12). Variations in touch will cause the harmonics to change constantly, certain harmonics becoming louder or fainter. The phenomenon applies to any note you play. I chose the low C for this example only because we've been working with it. We'll call the repeated note a *drone* or a *pedal point*.

EXAMPLE 4.12 A drone

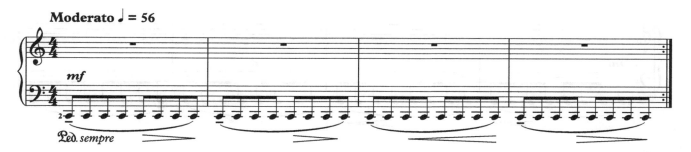

With changes in inflection, fingering, and dynamics, you can produce a hundred different colors and hues while repeating a single note a hundred times. "Axis Mundi" (example 4.13) is a one-note composition. To call a repeated note a composition is my most pretentious initiative yet. To give it a mystical-sounding name is doubly pretentious. Nevertheless, the repeated note well played on a freshly tuned acoustic instrument is, in fact, a portal to the expansion of consciousness. You can play the whole thing using the same finger repeatedly or alternating fingers.

Creative Health for Pianists

EXAMPLE 4.13 "Axis Mundi"

The Harmonics of "Celeste"

I wrote down the first six harmonics of the fundamentals of "Celeste" (example 4.14). Remember that the fundamental is also the first harmonic of its own series. The fundamentals are written normally, and harmonics two through six are written as diamond-head notes.

EXAMPLE 4.14 The harmonics of "Celeste"

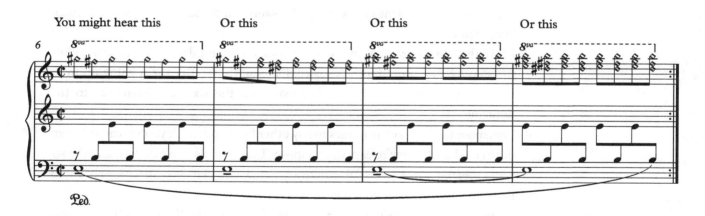

Your sounded harmonics depend on the instrument you're using, how well tuned it is, the acoustics of the room, your touch and timing. And your perception of harmonics also depends on multiple factors: chemicals in your blood stream, how fatigued or rested you are, your frame of mind, your posture. All these factors interact, and you may or may not hear the harmonics when you do our exercises. You can't force yourself to hear harmonics; you can only become receptive, the better to welcome whichever sounds come your way.

Your field of perception is subject to expansion and contraction. Visiting a friend, you notice a painting on the living room wall and you comment on it. "Ah, very nice! When did you get it?" Your friend answers, "It's been there for fifteen years. You sat under it just last week."

Your field of visual perception finally expands and takes in what was there all along. This is only a little example; the phenomenon is big, and it affects all of us. What we see, hear, feel, smell, sense, or appreciate is only a fraction of what we could potentially see, hear, and appreciate.

Play "Celeste" on a repeating loop. Sit upright and relaxed, don't look at your hands, enjoy the bouncy keyboard that stimulates your fingers, play and listen, play and listen. The repetitive performance plus the simplicity of "Celeste" might put you in some sort of trance, which is a letting-go of worries and judgments. And then you might finally hear harmonics in all their glory, the mysterious echoes and oscillations that were there all along.

Afterward, practice the "Celeste" variations that perhaps you found boring when you first met them. They, too, will become mysterious and magical.

For Lovers of Homework

As a pianist and musician, how much do you need to know about harmonics? You're the boss of your own needs. This section is for those of you who decide that studying harmonics in greater depth is worth your while. The exercise trains your ears and your analytical mind. Above all, the exercise enhances your capacity to listen to sonic textures—in chords, passages, pieces, and improvisations—and discern relationships, consonances and dissonances, sympathetic resonances, caresses and clashes.

1. Learn the first *six* harmonics, down cold, for the fundamental C.
2. Learn the first *eight* harmonics, down cold, for the fundamental C. You'll have to accept that the seventh harmonic can't be reproduced exactly on the piano keyboard. In the example, I added a down-pointing arrow to the seventh harmonic, indicating that it's much flatter than the written note played at the piano. Strictly speaking, the fifth harmonic is also a bit lower than the same note played in equal temperament.
3. Learn the first *sixteen* harmonics, down cold, for the fundamental C. If you follow the step-by-step procedure, it's easier than you think. Play them going up from the fundamental, and going back down from the sixteenth harmonic to the fundamental.
4. Transpose the first *six* harmonics to any other fundamental. If you've learned them down cold for C, they're easy to transpose. The intervals don't change, and the six notes together form a musical structure your ears quickly recognize: a tonic chord that sits comfortably in your hands.
5. Transpose the first *eight* harmonics to any fundamental. If you did the previous step, this one is pretty easy.
6. Transpose the first *sixteen* harmonics to any fundamental. By now you have all the information you need to accomplish this task.

Example 4.15 offers an abbreviation of the process: six harmonics, eight harmonics, and sixteen harmonics for the fundamental C; plus the start of the transposition process, in this case using the fundamental F.

EXAMPLE 4.15 Harmonics homework

Resonance and Voicing

By now you're getting used to my seemingly banal compositions that turn out to be not so banal once you start practicing them. Here's something that looks empty on paper, with a pretentious title as usual: "Distribuzione," which is Italian for distribution (example 4.16). If possible, practice it in on a well-tuned, fully open acoustic piano in a resonant room. The left hand plays the fundamental, and the right hand plays various combinations of pitches that correspond to harmonics. Touch and timing create nuances of resonance, or distributions of vibrations and oscillations.

After you play it as written, transpose everything one octave down and play it again. Or transpose the left hand down one or two octaves, leaving the right hand where it is. If you like homework, transpose the piece to any other key. And if you really like homework, learn to recognize the pitches in the right hand as harmonics you can number. For instance, when the right hand first comes into action it sounds harmonics 2 and 3. And if you really, really like homework, let "Distribuzione" be the fairy godmother of some of your improvisations and compositions.

EXAMPLE 4.16 "Distribuzione" ©Pedro de Alcantara

Creative Health for Pianists

EXAMPLE 4.16 Continued

Hymn to the Pedal

"Hymn to the Pedal" is a simple but effective exercise-composition that heightens your awareness of how the right pedal transforms a musical text (example 4.17).

EXAMPLE 4.17 "Hymn to the Pedal" ©Pedro de Alcantara

Play the pattern over and over. Vary its dynamics and articulations. In my youth I attended a recital by the Cuban pianist Jorge Bolet (1914–1990). On a piece by Franz Liszt, Bolet performed a very gradual crescendo that, in my memory, lasted two minutes. The reality may have been different, but the emotion was one of astonishment at such dynamic control, the feeling of infinity and eternity: a crescendo that goes on forever and ever.

Use the right pedal as a sort of added instrument. Vary the pedal's timing and pressure: short bursts, sustained bursts, half-pedal, sudden changes, gradual changes. Depending on how you play the pedal, you might create a shimmering, growling soundscape where individual notes meld and disappear. Once you start mixing and matching what you do with your hands with what you do with your foot, the nuances and effects at your disposal are vast.

Video Clip 17, "Hymn to the Pedal."

One of the principles from "Hymn to the Pedal" merits highlighting. The pattern of notes is unchanging; the use of the pedal is ever-changing. Let's call the notes *fixed*, and the use of the pedal *mobile*. In music and in life, the interaction between fixed elements and mobile elements pretty much determines what's going on. If you want to control the workings of a situation and its outcome, you need to master the combination of fixity and mobility within the situation. In its basic version, "Hymn to the Pedal" allows you to practice this all-important skill.

Once you get the hang of combining handwork with footwork, start varying the notes of the pattern itself—that is, start improvising and composing. An atonal and random improvisation is easy: a kind of playful banging in which anything goes. A structured improvisation with the potential to transform itself into an enduring composition is harder. But you're the boss of easy and hard in your life.

Clashes and Caresses

In any piece you play, the sonic edifice of relationships and hierarchies is created from the bottom up. The lowest pitch in a texture or chord dictates qualities of resonance, consonance, and dissonance.

In example 4.18, we hear the interval of the perfect fourth "E A" (1) as a dissonance: the A clashes with the fifth harmonic of the E, which happens to be a G♯. When we add a C below those two pitches (2), our ears stop focusing on the perfect fourth and, instead, capture the intervals "C E" and "C A," respectively a major third (3) and a major sixth (4), both of which we hear as consonances. We now consider the entire chord as consonant. But if we transform the chord by putting the C above the E and A (5), the dissonance comes to the fore again, and we consider the new chord as tonally unstable, even though it uses the same pitches as the consonant chord (2). Simplifying it, we'll say that music is a series of caresses and clashes among fundamentals and their harmonics, with the bottom note of any texture playing a determining role.

EXAMPLE 4.18 Intervallic relationships

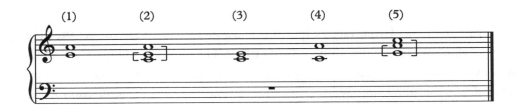

We'll study three pieces build on a left-hand drone, illustrating the primacy of the bottom note. "Forest Stone" is technically comfortable, allowing you to concentrate on touch, timing, inflection, voicing, and pedaling (example 4.19). In video clip 18 I play a short excerpt from it, in two versions with different tempi.

 Video Clip 18, "Forest Stone."

EXAMPLE 4.19 "Forest Stone" ©Pedro de Alcantara

EXAMPLE 4.19 Continued

EXAMPLE 4.19 Continued

"Grace" is a cousin of "Forest Stone," but with a richer right-hand life (example 4.20). On purpose, I employ a modular framework: a series of clearly delineated phrases, most of them four or eight bars long. This makes it easier for you to pick and choose among the phrases, to delete some or many, and to add your own.

EXAMPLE 4.20 "Grace" ©Pedro de Alcantara

EXAMPLE 4.20 Continued

EXAMPLE 4.20 Continued

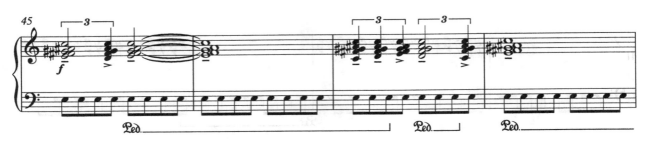

EXAMPLE 4.20 Continued

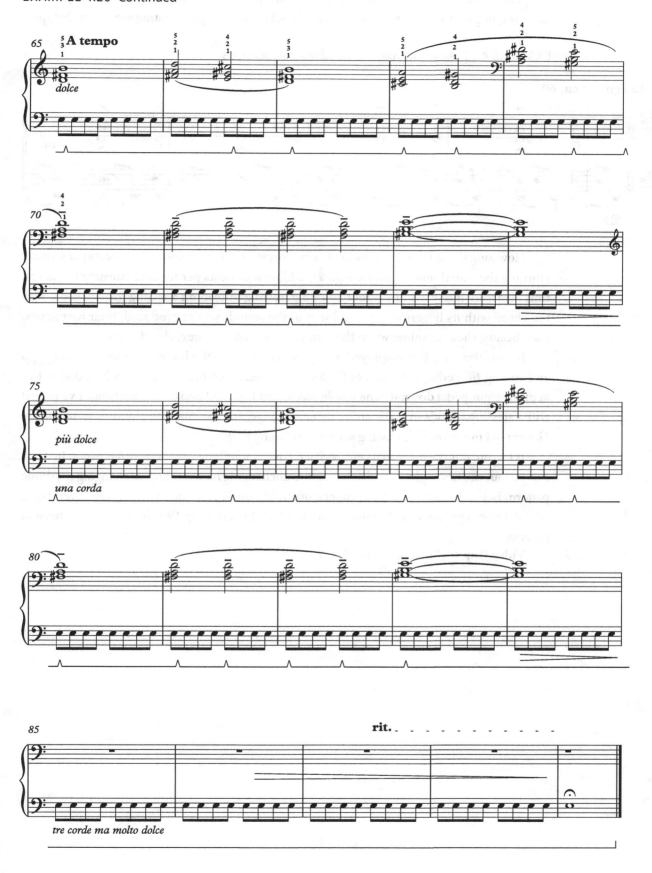

"Pacific Sunrise" has a seemingly placid surface, but close listening will show you that more is going on than meets the eye. Example 4.21 shows its germinating seed or archetype.

EXAMPLE 4.21 An archetype of sympathetic relationships

How long should the fermata last? I've performed the piece adding three beats per fermata (turning the actual time signature into $^6_2$); adding four beats per fermata (turning the actual time signature into $^7_2$); and without counting, relying instead on a feeling for vibration. Play the chord with its lingering fermata; listen to the sounds you've produced, their harmonics, their beauty, their meaning; when the time is right, strike the next chord and listen anew.

In performance, I've employed a long crescendo over the life of the piece, starting *ppp* and ending *fff*. Perhaps this makes for a clichéd interpretation, but it works beautifully. I've kept the right pedal down for the whole piece, and I've used pedaling gradations. I've played with caressing sounds over the entire dynamic range, and I've made the louder chords harsh. Generally I much prefer caressing sounds, including in *fff*.

If I wrote out the piece in its entirety, it'd cover something like six or seven pages. Instead, I wrote out the first eight bars, displaying the unchanging bass line and unchanging rhythmic pattern. Below it, I laid out the sequence of chords you'll play above the pattern. Everything is under your eyes on a single page (example 4.22). In video clip 19 I show you the pattern in practice.

▶ Video Clip 19, "Pacific Sunrise."

EXAMPLE 4.22 "Pacific Sunrise" ©Pedro de Alcantara

Sonic Sculpting

With little "Celeste" as my starting point, I created a composition highlighting the caresses and clashes of vibrant sounds. I call it "Celestial: In Memoriam ABM" (example 4.23). I've performed it with the pedal down from beginning to end, employing rubato, dynamics, and inflections to prevent sounds from piling up too much; and I've performed it with a more disciplined pedal. I like creating a vibrant loudness without banging at the piano. I like sitting upright and relatively still, and playing without looking at my hands as much as possible. I believe this improves both my playing and my hearing. I like playing with the piano lid fully open, and I like looking far into the space in front of my eyes. It probably puts me in some sort of trance-like state. The beginning of the composition might look a bit hairy from a counting perspective. You could retain the four pitches that I use and simply improvise a preluding arpeggio before launching into the main structure. In video clip 20 I practice the beginning of the piece. Example 4.24 is an aide-mémoire for the performance of the piece, its basic information fitted onto one page. It goes like this:

1. A preluding improvisation.
2. Four bars of a repeated A.
3. An eight-bar section played fourteen times with the indicated chord changes, but with an unchanging rhythmic structure.
4. A concluding improvisation.

▶ Video Clip 20, "Sonic Sculpting."

EXAMPLE 4.23 "Celestial: In Memoriam ABM" ©Pedro de Alcantara

EXAMPLE 4.23 Continued

EXAMPLE 4.23 Continued

Creative Health for Pianists

EXAMPLE 4.23 Continued

EXAMPLE 4.23 Continued

Creative Health for Pianists

EXAMPLE 4.24 An aide-mémoire for "ABM" ©Pedro de Alcantara

THE CIRCLE 5

Compositions
- Geek (example 5.4)
- Émile (example 5.7)
- Archimedes (example 5.8)
- Dodecahedron (example 5.11)
- Nadia (example 5.14)
- The Twelve Crying Princes (example 5.27)

Video Clips
21. The Circle of Fifths
22. The Skills of Transposition

Before anything else, let me tell you that I've created an appendix for readers interested in practicing the circle of fifths. The appendix takes some of the materials from this chapter and displays them in sequences that follow a counterclockwise path around the circle.

We begin our discussion with an archetypal journey starting and ending in C (example 5.1). If you're a beginner, you'll have to practice it multiple times until you get its feeling and memorize its information. If you're an experienced musician, "you know it already," but I'm inviting you to meet this sequence as if for the first time. Rediscovery is a pleasure sometimes more intense than discovery.

EXAMPLE 5.1 The circle of fifths

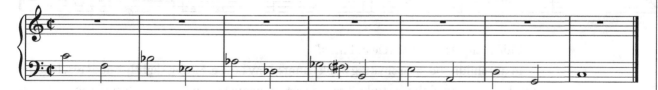

We get from C to C through an alternation of descending perfect fifths and ascending perfect fourths. Example 5.2 shows an alternative path, with a different ordering of fourths and fifths.

Creative Health for Pianists

EXAMPLE 5.2 A different sequence of fourths and fifths

The journey passes through all the notes of the chromatic scale, organized not as a series of semitones but as a series of descending fifths. To make it easier to grasp, to play, and to enjoy, we traditionally apply octave transpositions to some of these notes generated by descending fifths. Example 5.3 shows you a one-octave chromatic scale, its rearrangement in an unbroken sequence of descending fifths along the keyboard, and its further rearrangement using octave transpositions to achieve the familiar form. Strange as it may seem to the naked eye, all three versions use the exact same notes, but differently arrayed.

EXAMPLE 5.3 Three versions of the same sequence

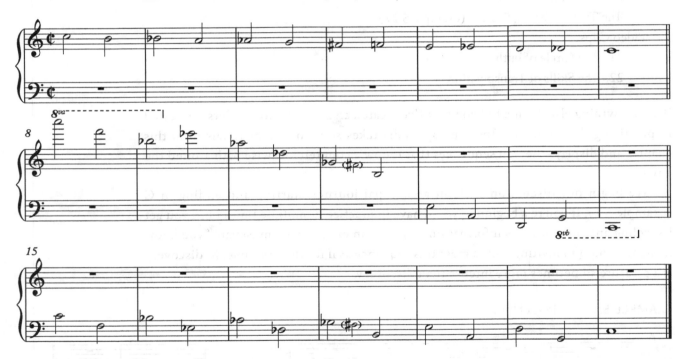

Video Clip 21, "The Circle of Fifths."

In my childhood, a fascinating book haunted my house. Sitting slightly out of reach in the bookshelves of my father's study, it was a sort of manual of anatomy, with superposed transparent plastic sheets showing the naked body, the muscular system, the vascular system, the nervous system, and the skeleton, one after the other. You could zero in on the skin, on the flesh, on the bones, on the nerves. And you could begin to appreciate the complexity of the living organism in its interrelated dimensions.

To discover the complexity of any one thing (of the human body, for instance) is to discover complexity itself. It's a deep and necessary lesson. It allows you to understand that the surface hides riches which you can't ever finish excavating. It doesn't matter how long you study the human body; you'll never have a complete, definitive picture of it in which you see all dimensions at the same time. This applies to the body, the brain, art, nature, mathematics, astrophysics, metaphysics, and a thousand other complex entities.

The circle of fifths is one of those ungraspable entities. It's a concept of such power and importance that we can't ever really own it. In my view, this is a good thing: it allows for infinite exploration.

The Circle of Fifths

We're ready for the circle of fifths in its graphic form (figure 5.1). Look at the outside circle, with capital letters. Follow the circle counterclockwise and you'll recognize the sequence of pitches in example 5.1.

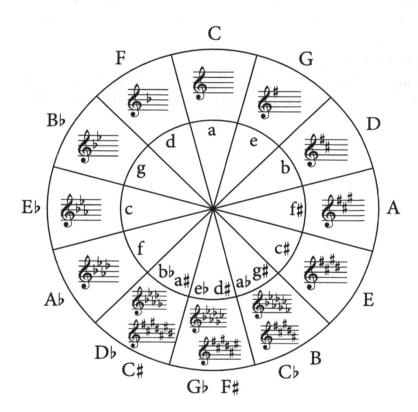

FIGURE 5.1 The circle of fifths

The amount of information in figure 5.1 is staggering. Letters displayed in two separate circles, one sequence in upper case, one sequence in lower case; a circle with twelve segments, showing sharps and flats in increasing numbers; three of those segments containing double information, with both flats and sharps in alarming numbers. The more you look, the more you see. You could die of anxiety or happiness, depending on how you react to it. And you might become *very anxious* if I tell you that you must, you *really must* understand and memorize *every last bit of information* in this figure.

Faced with something that's too much for you, simplify it into a form you can cope with. Then, add layers of information one by one. It's the same principle of the anatomy book of my youth. Figure 5.2 shows six layers of information, displayed over two pages. You can understand it all visually, without reading a description of the various layers. But if you like your images to have subtitles, as it were, here they are:

1. Nothing but a circle. You can draw it easily, for instance tracing it with the help of a CD or a cereal bowl.
2. The same circle, marked with twelve points at regular intervals like the face of a clock.
3. The same circle, now indicating twelve pitches separated by perfect fifths, with three of those pitches receiving a double identity (sharp and flat). The pitches are annotated in upper case, indicating major keys.
4. Another circle with twelve pitches along the inside of the circle, and as before three pitches have double identities. The pitches are annotated in lower case, indicating minor keys.
5. Circles #3 and 4, juxtaposed.
6. The major and minor keys, with key signatures added. It allows you to see, for instance, that the keys of A major and F♯ minor both have three sharps. Very helpful!

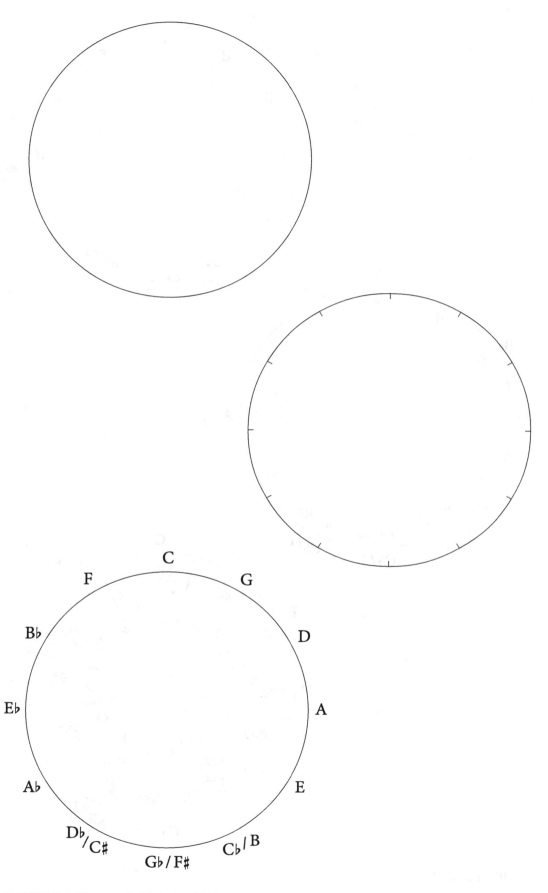

FIGURE 5.2 The manifold circle of fifths

Creative Health for Pianists

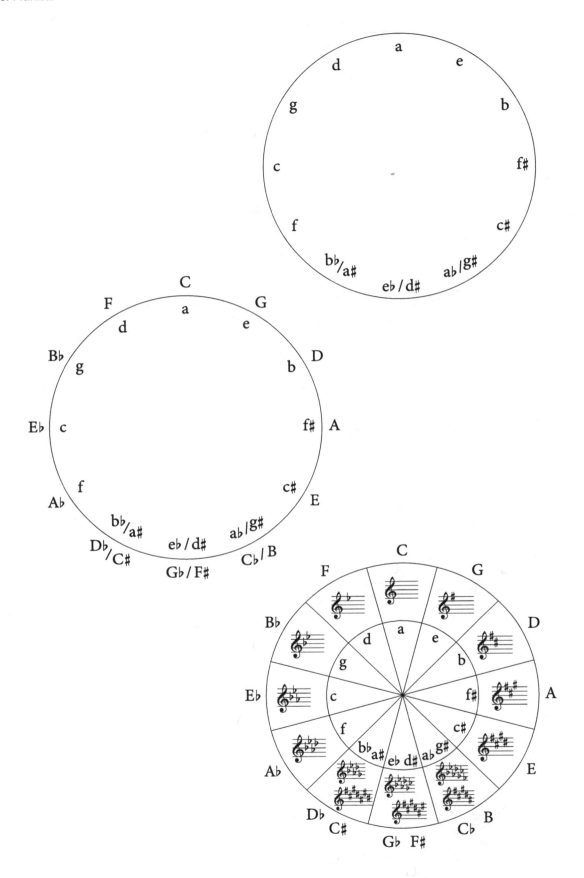

FIGURE 5.2 Continued

Relationships within the Circle of Fifths

The information in the circle of fifths is dizzyingly rich. We'll take the letter C as an illustration. It stands for a pitch class, meaning every C that you can play or sing, regardless of how high or how low. It also stands for the root of the C-major chord—that is, the chord that uses C, E, and G in various combinations. It also stands for a tonality: C major itself, the center of a sonic territory that could delineate a whole composition, for instance Schubert's Ninth Symphony (known as "Great"), D. 944 in C major. There are other dimensions to this C of ours, but for now we'll content ourselves to listing *pitch*, *chord*, and *tonality* as aspects of its identity, all implicit in the circle of fifths.

The circle takes two relationships into account: the movement by perfect fifth clock- and counterclockwise, and the movement by minor third between the outer and inner circles. Let's suppose you'll use the key of C major as a starting point. Move clockwise along the outer circle, and your first stop is G. Move counterclockwise, and your first stop is F. We'll name G the *dominant* of C, and F the *subdominant* of C. Going from the outer to the inner circle, C major is paired with A minor, which we call the *relative minor* of C major. Logically, we call C major the *relative major* of A minor.

These relationships are note-to-note relationships, chord-to-chord relationships, and functional relationships within phrases and entire compositions. For instance, the first movement of a sonata by Mozart might be in C major; the second movement, slower in tempo and more lyrical, might be in F major. Simplifying, we'll say that moving counterclockwise along the circle of fifths brings the feeling of a drop or descent or relaxation; moving clockwise brings the feeling of something going up, rising in tension.

The language and style of a composer is partly determined by the paths that his or her compositions take along the circle of fifths. Antonio Vivaldi (1678–1741) travels cautiously along the circle of fifths. Writing a movement for one of his concertos, he chooses a starting point—D minor, for instance—and stays within its immediate neighborhood, perhaps visiting F major, B♭ major, and G minor in the course of the movement. Gustav Mahler (1860–1911) chooses the same starting point of D minor, but he travels far along the circle of fifths, perhaps visiting distant keys like A♭ major or C♯ minor. Hearing one of Mahler's compositions would give Vivaldi a heart attack.

You can set out to memorize these relationships by thinking and by sensing. When thinking, you look at the information on paper, you count tones and semitones, you add sharps and flats, and you use words to name intervals and relationships. When sensing, you listen and play, play and sing. Listeners without any musical training enjoy a song on the radio, often memorizing the song after one or two tries. It's hardly possible for a song not to employ aspects of the circle of fifths in its construction. It means that untrained listeners have their own response (primarily sensorial, and secondarily intellectual) to the circle of fifths.

Neuroscience probably has things to say about how navigating the circle of fifths affects the brain: it makes you feel good, and there must be brain waves and dopamine involved. Theology, too, probably has things to say about how navigating the circle of fifths affects the soul: it gives you a sense of order, coherence, direction, meaning, and infinite combinatorial possibilities. The metaphysically inclined won't fail to notice the symbolic implications of the number twelve: the twelve pitches of the chromatic scale and the twelve points along the circle of fifths; the twelve months, the twelve signs of the zodiac; the twelve members of a jury; the twelve Olympians, the twelve tribes of Israel, the twelve apostles. To study the circle of fifths is to sense the organizational, transcendent power of the number twelve (figure 5.3).

FIGURE 5.3 The cathedral at Chartres

The Enharmonic Passage

Example 5.4 shows two notes sounding the perfect fifth C-G, followed by a number of strange-looking intervals. If you play the sequence at the piano, you'll simply repeat the same, unchanging pitches from beginning to end! Let's be silly and call it a conceptual composition, with the title "Geek."

EXAMPLE 5.4 "Geek"

Depending on context, I'm called Pedro, Mr. de Alcantara, Monsieur Alcantara, honey, and other names still. Either I'm many different people, or I'm a single entity to which observers attach varied names according to their assessment of how best to address me. I'm not called "honey" across every situation in my life.

Depending on context, a certain sound is called a G♯ or an A♭ or an F𝄪, although all three pitches are played on the same key at the piano and sound exactly alike. Such pitches are called *enharmonically equivalent.* Intervals also depend on context. The same two notes played together might be called a perfect fifth, a diminished sixth, or a double-augmented fourth, as illustrated in "Geek." These intervals are also considered enharmonically equivalent.

Traveling along the circle of fifths, at some point you'll pass from the territory of flats (represented, for instance, by E♭ major and C minor, both of which have three flats) to the territory of sharps (for instance, A major and F♯ minor, both of which have three sharps). In between those two territories, there's a strip of land that's ambiguous, because it belongs to both the flat and the sharp territories.

The enharmonic passage—that is, the voyage from the world of flats to the world of sharps and vice-versa—contains a visual component that can be confusing. Example 5.5 introduces you to an illustration of this passage. If you aren't familiar with the phenomenon, your eyes risk disliking what they see and preventing you from understanding it. Let's work through it.

EXAMPLE 5.5 The enharmonic passage

1. "This looks weird. The intervals don't make sense. F♭ to D♯ is insane. It's probably atonal, or very modern at any rate. It must sound funny."
2. If you lived in a world of flats only, you'd see this. The intervals would be easy to read.
3. If you lived in a world of sharps only, you'd see this. The intervals would be equally easy to read.
4. You're passing from the world of flats to the world of sharps. There are equivalencies among notes from each world. Let's make the equivalencies explicit with the little notes in parenthesis.
5. "Okay, I see what's happening. I can probably cope with it now. It's neither modern nor atonal nor dissonant nor weird nor out of my zone of comfort."

The Counterclockwise Journey

The circle of fifths is like a map of a town with twenty-four monuments. You can go from monument to monument at random, or you can design a sequence with a logical pattern. Going back and forth, visiting a monument more than once, lingering by a monument or skipping one or more monuments: the number of possible journeys within this town is gigantic. Here we'll consider one of these journeys: the steady travel counterclockwise along the outside circle. If you start with C, the first destination will be F. Then comes B♭, then E♭, and so on.

For acoustic reasons, this is one of the most meaningful paths along the circle. Example 5.6 lays out the information you need to understand how it works.

EXAMPLE 5.6 The counterclockwise journey

1. When we play a C on the piano, we hear both the fundamental (the C itself) and its harmonic series. Example 5.6 starts by laying out the first eight harmonics for the fundamental C.
2. If we lay out these harmonics as a chord, we recognize a dominant seventh chord in the key of F.
3. Our ears consider that this chord is begging for resolution—that is, we want to hear a consonant F-major tonic chord after we hear the dominant seventh chord.

4. Here's the problem. When we hear the F-major chord, the harmonic series of the fundamental F again create a dominant seventh chord, now in the key of B♭ major. To our ears, it too begs for resolution!
5. Once we land on the B♭ major chord, we again hear a dominant seventh chord begging for resolution. You guessed right: this could go on forever and ever.
6. We'll lay out a journey that start with a sequence of these dominant seventh chords that never resolve.
7. And at some point we'll break the sequence with a chord that allows us to free ourselves from getting stuck in an obsessive loop of unresolved chords.

In sum, our ears find the counterclockwise travel along the circle of fifths deeply satisfying. Composers and improvisers have taken millions of these journeys, sometimes abridged, sometimes extended. And it doesn't matter if millions of journeys have already been taken. The path is forever green.

Example 5.7 lays out a series of sequences like a little travelogue. I'll deem it a composition and give it the title "Émile" in homage to an old friend of mine, the pianist, improviser, and composer Émile Naoumoff. Here's a brief description of its contents:

1. The twelve pitches of the chromatic scale, plus a finishing touch.
2. The circle of fifths, plus a finishing touch.
3. The interaction of the chromatic scale and the circle of fifths. This creates an alternation of major thirds and minor sevenths.
4. The addition of a second chromatic scale. This creates the famous sequence of never-resolving seventh chords.
5. The alteration of every second chord by lowering its third. The resulting sequence alternates major-third and minor-third chords.
6. The lowering of the thirds of every chord. The resulting sequence is uniformly made of minor-third chords.
7. The same as the previous sequence, with different articulations.

Creative Health for Pianists

EXAMPLE 5.7 "Émile"

EXAMPLE 5.7 Continued

Strictly speaking, there are three variations on the counterclockwise journey: all twelve major keys; all twelve minor keys; or all major and minor keys in alternation, for a total of twenty-four keys. The latter would go like this: C major, A minor; F major, D minor; B♭ major, G minor; and so on. The appendix includes a couple of trips based on this alternation of major and minor keys.

The Circle of Fifths Progression

The circle of fifths is built on the twelve pitches of the chromatic scale, arranged as a sequence of descending perfect fifths. What happens if instead we limit ourselves to the seven pitches of a diatonic major scale and arrange them as a sequence of fifths? The sequence will be shorter, of course; and, importantly, one of the fifths will be diminished instead of perfect. This sequence receives many names, including *the diatonic circle of fifths* and the *circle of fifths progression*. Example 5.8 lays out various layers of information related to it. I'll deem it a composition and title it "Archimedes."

1. The major scale.
2. Its rearrangement into fifths.
3. The progression as a series of triads.
4. The same progression, with added sevenths (which intensifies the progression's forward momentum).
5. The basic progression, in minor.
6. The progression, with added sevenths, starting in C major and ending in A minor with a cadential formula.

A tonality may have several chords in common with another tonality. C major and A minor, for instance, have six out of seven chords in common. It makes it easy to pivot from key to key, with only one change of accidental. When Archimedes understood the principle of shared chords among different tonalities, he exclaimed "Eureka!" The circle of fifths progression is amazingly flexible, and a favorite of composers across eras and styles.

If you like homework, learn to transpose the progression to all major and minor keys. Once you get the hang of C major and A minor, other keys aren't that difficult to play by ear, or to build up methodically: start with a scale, rearrange it as a left-hand progression moving by fifths, add right-hand chords. But if you prefer to read the progressions off a score, you'll find them in the appendix, where I wrote out the progression in all major and minor keys.

EXAMPLE 5.8 "Archimedes"

Seemingly Strange Accidentals

Why would a composer use a key signature of four sharps for a few bars, only to change the key to six flats immediately afterward? What's the point of a double sharp or a double flat? Why can't I just rewrite every B♯ as a C♮, or to call every B♭ an A♯?

Musical notation follows logical rules. The rules, which are many, interact in complex ways that can seem confusing before you work them out. Once you wrap your brain around these rules, you'll see the merits of seemingly strange accidentals like those dreaded double flats and double sharps. The subject of accidentals is too vast; here I'd like to give you a simple but definitive illustration. Play the little diddle in example 5.9, which you'll recognize it right away.

EXAMPLE 5.9 The famous diddle

One reason why the diddle is eternally popular, and eternally irritating to the ear, is the presence of *tendency tones* (which we first met in chapter 3). We really, really want the F♯ in the first bar to go back to G; and we really, really want the A♭ in the second bar also to resolve to G. Both these chromatic alterations are *tending* toward a destination. Tendency tones aren't necessarily chromatic. Just before the end of the diddle, the tritone F-B practically begs to be resolved to the minor-sixth E-C: the F tends to E, the B tends to C. Tendency tones are at the heart of tonal music and the interplay of tension and relaxation, dissonance and consonance, harmony and counterpoint.

Let's transpose the diddle to D♭ major (example 5.10). Following the rules of musical notation, we must—we *must*!—use a B♭♭. It allows us to grasp the relationships between pitches right away, because we see that the B♭♭ is a tendency tone that "wants to resolve" downward to the A♭. In this context, using an A♮ would be visually and musically absurd.

EXAMPLE 5.10 A tendency tone

I invite you to play the diddle in twelve keys, traveling counterclockwise along the circle of fifths (example 5.11). You'll meet a B♭ that isn't an A♯, an E♯ that isn't an F, a B♯ that isn't a C, a C♭ that isn't a B, and an F♭ that isn't an E. In the Appendix, I display the same sequence without key signature changes, for ease of learning. I'll call the sequence a composition, with the very pretentious title "Dodecahedron." Playing it is like telling the same joke twelve times in a row (thirteen, since I repeat the C major joke at the end). Tempo, timing, inflection, dynamics . . . it's never boring.

EXAMPLE 5.11 "Dodecahedron"

I'd like to share a useful tool with you: a section of the piano keyboard in multiple versions, with the keys named in ever more complex ways (figure 5.4). You'll see that the same note is called by different names. It's easy to sense this by looking at the black keys: we immediately comprehend that a certain key can play either an F♯ or a G♭. It's less easy to sense that *every* key at the keyboard (with one exception) can be any of *three* notes. And some of these notes are, indeed, double sharps and double flats. Musical context will determine whether the composer needs to write a G, an F𝄪, or an A♭♭.

Depending on your level of piano playing and the sort of repertory you play, you might never encounter a ♭♭ or a 𝄪. But you're better off acknowledging their existence, and their reason for existing.

1. We start with a diagram of the piano keys over one octave. This is the keyboard as you see it on your piano.
2. We add note names to the white keys.
3. We add note names to the black keys. It doesn't shock us to see that each black key has two names, two functions, two identities.
4. The white keys on the piano also have multiple identities and functions. Here we add a few of these multiple identities.
5. We now discover every identity for every key. Perhaps to our surprise, we see that almost all keys on the piano have not just two, but three identities, some of them involving double flats and double sharps. Psychologically, this information could feel like a threat: foreign, incomprehensible, out of reach. To begin with, look at it graphically and visually, without trying to understand it. It becomes an interesting little work of art or design. It might remain musically incomprehensible to you, but it isn't a threat anymore. Once you get rid of the fear, you can start learning your double flats and double sharps over the days, weeks, and months. Or... don't bother with it. Stay with version #4 of the keyboard, or version #3, or any other version that suits you.
6. Let's strip the keyboard of those pesky double flats and sharps. This version is the same as version #3. We're relaxing and going back to relative safety.
7. This is the same as version #2: white keys named. Easy, right?
8. This is the same as version #1. No names, only the familiar keyboard. Imagine, sense, remember, and know that the simple keyboard contains a wealth of complex relationships.

The Circle

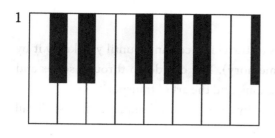
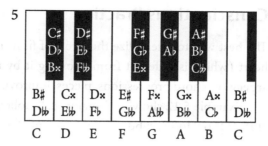
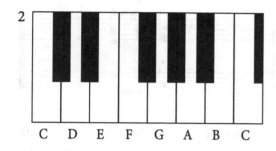
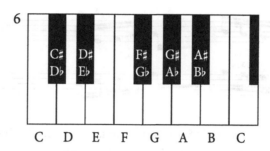
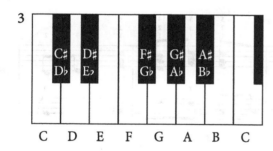
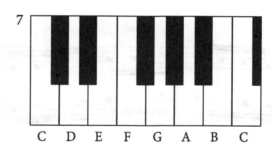
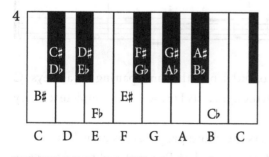
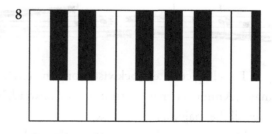

FIGURE 5.4 Layers of the keyboard

Creative Health for Pianists

Conscientious Practice

The best way to internalize the circle of fifths is to travel it incessantly, until you know it by heart (which is different from knowing it by memory). You can do so through scales and arpeggios, chord progressions, pieces, improvisations, and the art of transposition.

Example 5.12 shows a C-major scale, followed by a simple chord sequence that we'll call "I IV V I" or "tonic, subdominant, dominant, tonic."

EXAMPLE 5.12 A scale and a chord progression

Example 5.13 shows the same materials, slightly speeded up and followed by their version in A minor, using the ascending melodic minor scale and the descending natural minor scale.

EXAMPLE 5.13 Major and minor

Traveling counterclockwise along the circle of fifths, play the same pairing for all keys: C major, A minor; F major, D minor; and onward. In the appendix I present the complete journey over all the major and minor keys.

Example 5.14 eliminates the scales and gathers the chord progressions only. Is it a score or just a database? I'll say it's a composition and title it "Nadia." Play it straight, or use it as a stepping stone to variation and improvisation.

EXAMPLE 5.14 "Nadia"

EXAMPLE 5.14 Continued

In addition to practicing scales and progressions, decide that you'll improvise at least one little bit in every key, major and minor. Example 5.15 shows you how you might start this exploration.

EXAMPLE 5.15 At least one little bit

An Introduction to Transposition

It's been said that there are no advanced techniques, only advanced applications of basic techniques. Transposing a simple piece of music to a neighboring key is simple; transposing a complex piece to a distant key is complex. But both are applications of the same technique.

Transpose the middle C up by a diatonic semitone. Sure, D♭. Child's play.

Transpose the middle C up by a minor thirteenth. Ouch! Something is now intimidating you: the writer of this book, your piano teacher, the composer, the piano itself, math, white and black keys, the threat of humiliation and shame. In truth, you're being called to do two things: confront a situation you find intimidating, and transpose a pitch up a minor thirteenth. It's not a banal exercise.

Counting is good. Looking things up on the internet is good. Educated guesses are good, particularly if you make the distinction between "I'm guesstimating" and "I know for a fact." Correcting yourself quickly when you discover you're in error, that's good, too. To be afraid of something for no good reason . . . that's not so good (example 5.16).

Creative Health for Pianists

EXAMPLE 5.16 Transposing by counting

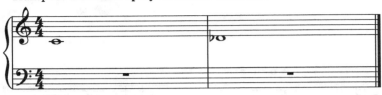

"Phew. Minor 13th."

Being straightforward and mostly diatonic, the materials of *Creative Health for Pianists* usually lend themselves to the practice of transposition without too much difficulty. Their mathematics are simple, and they give you time and space to find a helpful frame of mind in which to transpose. To develop this skill, we'll employ four of our archetypal snippets: "Celeste" (chapter 4), "In Estonia" (chapter 3), "Dialogue" (chapter 1), and "Heartbreak" (chapter 2).

Transposing a simple three-note, two-pitch pattern like "Celeste" is only slightly harder than transposing a single note. Example 5.17 shows the first few "Celeste" transpositions counterclockwise along the circle of fifths, starting in the original key of E.

EXAMPLE 5.17 Transposing "Celeste"

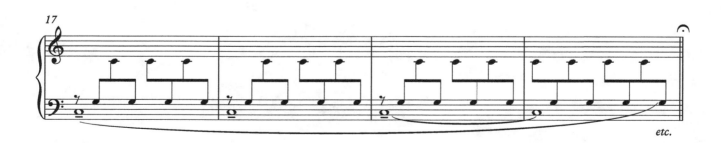

Creative Health for Pianists

Your hands take on a shape according to the key you're playing. The hands of C major aren't shaped the same way as hands of E♭ major or F♯ minor. This may seem obvious, but if you haven't had this thought you may be missing out on one of the tools of transposition (and also of improvisation and composition). A tonality is a path through the keyboard. Valleys and hills are shaped one way in C major, another in E♭ major. And your hands shape and reshape themselves as you navigate the white and black keys through flats and sharps, double flats and double sharps.

The next exercise shows "Celeste" transpositions that don't follow the closest-neighbor route along the circle of fifths. The tonal changes are more jagged. Let a friend of yours shout a key at you, any key! And you play "Celeste" in the shouted key. Example 5.18 shows a few tonalities chosen more or less at random.

EXAMPLE 5.18 Transposing to random keys

You might like to revisit "Celeste: Theme and Variations" from chapter 4. They provide you with challenges of transposition slightly greater than the "Celeste" snippet in isolation. Let your shouting friend attend your piano recital, and ask him to shout a key and a variation for you to play on the spot. Variation II in F♯! Variation V in A♭! Failing that, play the variations in any order you wish, each variation in any key you wish. Or think through a tonal sequence that makes sense to you.

Now we revisit "In Estonia" (from chapter 3). Example 5.19 reminds you of how it starts.

EXAMPLE 5.19 A reminder from "In Estonia"

The original is in E major, which is friendly to your pianistic hands. Practice the original in its entirety until you're so comfortable with the piece's rhythmic and melodic structure that you know it by heart. Then transpose it to C major, where you'll start the counterclockwise journey around the circle of fifths alternating each major key with its relative minor.

For our purposes, "In Estonia" is useful because it employs a single position, each hand playing only the first five notes of a diatonic scale. Example 5.20 shows you the five notes each hand will play in every major and minor key.

How to practice the sequence? It's up to you. Use the metronome and play every key in the absolute same way. Or interpret each key by varying tempo, dynamics, and inflections. Change registers and play a key up by one or more octaves, or down. Harder keys? Play them more slowly. Easier keys? You can play them more slowly, too.

Creative Health for Pianists

EXAMPLE 5.20 All 24 major and minor keys

Now let's transpose something a little more challenging: our old friend from chapter 1, "Dialogue." Example 5.21 refreshes your memory with one of the thousand possible variations of this archetype, here shown as ascending and descending scales.

EXAMPLE 5.21 A reminder from "Dialogue"

One way of transposing consists in inhabiting a new key in the company of your musical materials. Analytical calculations of flats and sharps are secondary to your sensing how the materials live and breathe in the new key. Let's try F major. You just "play with it" (example 5.22).

EXAMPLE 5.22 Play with it

"Dialogue" is built by juxtaposing sixths, although the fingerings we use make it seem that we're juxtaposing fifths. Find the scales in parallel sixths that you need to play in your target key (example 5.23).

EXAMPLE 5.23 Build it in steps

Do you still feel the need to be more certain of your sharps and flats? Give yourself a little reminder: "Every B must be flat; every B♭ is a black key" (example 5.24).

EXAMPLE 5.24 Pinpoint the needed changes

Go back and forth between a few chords that remind you that you're now in F major—in other words, chords that contain a B♭. You're training your hands and your ears together, thanks to musical materials that happen to be beautiful and pianist-friendly (example 5.25).

EXAMPLE 5.25 Focus on the new information

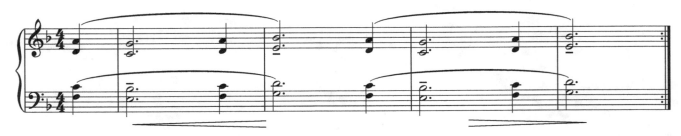

The fermata invites you to own space and time, to listen, to enjoy yourself. "What comes next? Which sounds and fingerings, which sharps or flats, which pleasures?" Each fermata lasts as long as you want it to last (example 5.26).

EXAMPLE 5.26 Use fermatas

You're not working on transposition per se; you're working on how you feel, think, breathe, and move when you're presented with the task of transposing something. It's a meditation in embodied mindfulness, in which the fermata suspends chronological time and gives you as much psychological time as you need to find your path forward.

Video Clip 22, "The Skills of Transposition."

How much effort will you put into learning these skills? For those readers who don't plan to do the work of transposing it, I wrote out a counterclockwise sequence employing the descending-scale version of "Dialogue." Example 5.27 lays it out. I'll deem it a composition and give it the title "The Twelve Crying Princes." I didn't include key signature changes, which means that all flats and sharps are marked right next to their notes. Choose a key, then play it back and forth with fermatas, with rhythmic variations, as if you were rewriting the entire "Dialogue" chapter in the key of your choosing. Then play all keys in sequence, lingering on each key with embellishments, variations, and improvisations. In the appendix, I show the same sequence with added key-signature changes.

Creative Health for Pianists

EXAMPLE 5.27 "The Twelve Crying Princes" ©Pedro de Alcantara

EXAMPLE 5.27 Continued

Now transpose "Heartbreak" from chapter 2. Example 5.28 reminds you of it. In the Appendix you'll find the transpositions written out, but here I invite you to spin them out for yourself.

EXAMPLE 5.28 A reminder from "Heartbreak"

There are twelve keys, each sweet and sad in its own way. Passing from one key to another is, in itself, a sweet and sad moment. Your manner of transposing a piece becomes your interpretation of the piece, in that moment. Determined or easy-going, thoughtful or rushed, indifferent or excited, heartfelt or coldblooded? Your attitude is an interpretation. To struggle at high speed is an interpretation; to think and feel at slow speed is an interpretation. To transpose "this exercise" is an interpretation; to transpose "this composition" is an interpretation. To transpose by calculation is an interpretation; to transpose by feeling is an interpretation. To transpose in fear is an interpretation; to transpose in love is an interpretation. The better to process the transposition, you decide to play it andante molto moderato, with multiple fermatas. These are both psychological and interpretive decisions. It'll be wonderfully heartbreaking to hear a pianist deliberately and cautiously transpose "Heartbreak" to a distant key with which the pianist isn't comfortable.

Imagine that you're doing your transposition homework in public. Or arrange your schedule so that you actually do it in public, in front of one or two friends or a small circle of like-minded musical explorers. Here's a famous proverb of uncertain origin: "When alone, behave as if in the presence of the master; when in the presence of the master, behave as if alone" (figure 5.5).

FIGURE 5.5 Count Basie

GESTURE 6

Compositions
- Sergei's Warm-up (example 6.5)
- Sergei (example 6.6)
- Sergei's Right (example 6.7)
- Amby (example 6.10)
- Light and Shadow (example 6.11)
- Respect (example 6.12)
- Obsedanta (example 6.14)
- Thimble (example 6.15)
- Empty Nest (example 6.16)
- Remorse (example 6.18)
- Mikro (example 6.20)
- Love Left (example 6.21)
- Envelope (example 6.22)
- Love Right (example 6.23)

Video Clips
23. The Crawler
24. Crossing Hands
25. Improvising to a Constraint
26. Singing Thumbs
27. Nested Thumbs

Brain and heart, body and soul, piano and pianist, gesture and music. This chapter gathers multiple tools to help you become aware of how these dimensions so interact as to be inseparable.

We start with the "Crawler." Let's quote the Four Musketeers: "All for one, and one for all!" (The famous novel by Alexandre Dumas is called *The Three Musketeers*, but in fact it consists of the musketeer d'Artagan telling the story of how he met the other three: Athos, Porthos, and Aramis.) In its basic version, the Crawler organizes the hand into two units: the thumb by itself, and the other four fingers acting as a fused totality (example 6.1). This has the effect of stabilizing the hand and giving it surprising strength: all for one, and one for all!

▶ Video Clip 23, "The Crawler."

EXAMPLE 6.1 The Crawler, first version

In its second version, the Crawler again organizes the hand into two units: the little finger by itself, the other fingers and the thumb as the fused totality (example 6.2).

Creative Health for Pianists

EXAMPLE 6.2 The Crawler, second version

Vary it, spice it up, improvise (example 6.3).

EXAMPLE 6.3 Crawler variations

You can "do the Crawler" in any context, adapting it to the notes, chords, and passages that you want to stabilize. We'll illustrate this with the "Seesaw" pattern from chapter 3 (example 6.4).

EXAMPLE 6.4 Adapting the Crawler

Adaptation, transformation, variation, improvisation, composition. We'll tweak the original "Crawler" by playing a scale in D♭ major, in alternation with four-note chords using the black keys above and adjacent to the scale note. This creates slightly asymmetrical note patterns. In the left-hand version, the little finger plays the scale; in the right-hand version, the thumb plays the scale. We'll call it a composition: "Sergei's Warm-up" (example 6.5).

EXAMPLE 6.5 "Sergei's Warm-up"

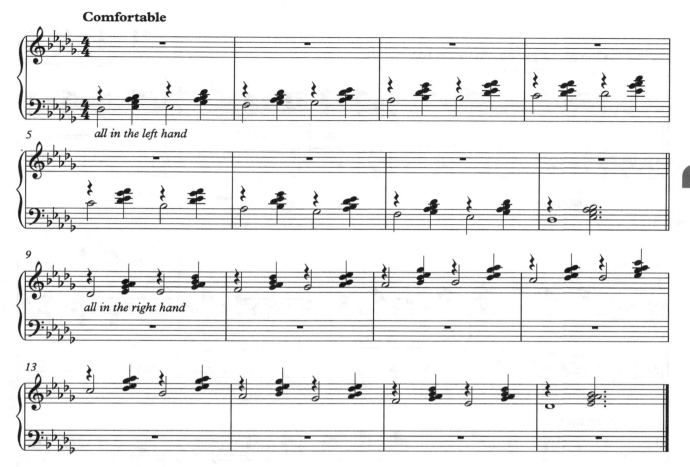

I tweaked the tweak and created a composition in D♭ major (example 6.6). Sight-reading it may be a little tricky, but playing it isn't too difficult. I've laid it out for the left hand and titled it "Sergei."

To play "Sergei" with the right hand, transpose it up one octave and use the logical, mirrored fingerings. In example 6.7 I laid it out for you, with a couple of small changes. But I suggest that you don't read my version; instead, do your own transposition, perhaps by ear after you learn the original version. Let's give this new version a compositional title: "Sergei's Right."

Like all exercises and compositions, "Sergei" lends itself to variation. In example 6.8 I wrote down a few possibilities.

1. I played everything as single chords, rather than a melody with syncopated chords as in the original.
2. The better to read and visualize the version of single chords, I rewrote it. It's the absolute same thing as the previous variation, except it's a lot easier to digest visually.
3. I arpeggiated the chords and changed the rhythms and the time signature.
4. I transposed the right-hand version an octave up, and slowed it down considerably. It sounds pretty, and it's easier to play.
5. I liberated myself from the constraints of the Crawler and I assigned the syncopated chords to the right hand, playing the piece with both hands. Why not?
6. I liberated myself from the constraints of lyricism and decided to play it bouncy and happy.

Creative Health for Pianists

EXAMPLE 6.6 "Sergei" ©Pedro de Alcantara

EXAMPLE 6.7 "Sergei's Right" ©Pedro de Alcantara

Creative Health for Pianists

EXAMPLE 6.8 Variations on "Sergei"

Crossing Hands

Example 6.9 is an extremely streamlined crossing-hands exercise—that is, an archetype. Using the right pedal, put it on a loop and enjoy the back-and-forth. Gradations of timing, dynamics, posture, and touch could keep you busy for a good while. And you don't have to obey the sequence of hand exchanges in the example; you can make up your own back-and-forth.

Video Clip 24, "Crossing Hands."

EXAMPLE 6.9 Crossing hands

Your left hand thinks and feels in a certain way, with its strengths and weaknesses. Among its habits, it sings the bass line, it plays the lowest notes in most textures, it imagines itself as part of the rhythm section in a jazz band. The right hand, too, has its habits, strengths, and weaknesses. It sings the melodies, it sounds the higher notes in most textures, it likes showing off. Simplifying it, the left hand is the bass, the baritone, and the tenor; and the right hand is the alto, the mezzo soprano, and the soprano.

The mere fact of crossing your hands at the piano upends everyone's habits.

The gesture's physicality is meaningful. The shoulders and the back get involved, the head and neck too. The crossing invites a balance of opposing forces, in which the "animal that is the right arm" playfully pulls your back leftward while "the animal that is the left arm" pulls your back rightward. Do it skillfully, and your body gains in strength and stability (figure 6.1).

FIGURE 6.1 Left and right

Dominant and non-dominant hands; masculine qualities and feminine qualities; right brain, left brain; orientation in space; thought, sensation, emotion. Crossing hands rearranges everything. It doesn't matter if your repertory doesn't call for crossing hands. You'll benefit a lot from practicing it often, and in varied styles.

Example 6.10 extends the archetype. It becomes a very modest composition, which I'll title "Amby."

EXAMPLE 6.10 "Amby"

Creative Health for Pianists

Example 6.11 spices things up a little. Let's call it "Light and Shadow."

EXAMPLE 6.11 "Light and Shadow" ©Pedro de Alcantara

The principle of crossing hands lends itself to infinite variations, improvisations, and compositions. The one requirement is for you to cross your hands in some way, at some point, at least once. Everything else is negotiable. Example 6.12 is a tiny, tiny composition with some lovely sympathetic resonances. It respects the one requirement (to cross the hands), and for this reason we must consider it a success and give it a title: "Respect." Its core is simple: one hand holds a chord, the other travels here and there. Do a sequence of changing chords, for instance, holding each for a while. Hold the chord with the left hand instead. Go atonal. Go wild.

EXAMPLE 6.12 "Respect"

Improvise to a Constraint

Improvising to a constraint isn't new to us. We've improvised to the constraints of "Dialogue," for instance, or "Heartbreak" among many others. Here we'll generalize and systematize the concept.

The constraint can be a musical prompt: use only the black keys. Or a physical prompt: cross your hands every three notes. It can be simple: play something, anything, in $\frac{3}{4}$. Or it can be complicated: the left hand placid like a still lake and playing in D major, the right hand on the verge of a nervous breakdown and playing in E♭ minor.

Quickly you'll see that every musical prompt is a physical prompt, and vice versa.

Strip "Happy Birthday" of its melody and lyrics, keeping only the rhythms and note values. Now improvise. This is only an illustrative example; improvise to any set rhythms, whether they come from an existing piece or not.

Tie your index and middle fingers together with rubber bands. Now play. Panic or pleasure?

Make the "OK" sign with your hands: a circle with index and thumb, the other fingers in free motion. Some note combinations will become impossible, others will arise logically from this particular constraint.

Cross your hands. How low can you play with the right hand, and how high can you play with the left hand at the same time? I managed a range of six octaves plus a semitone. If I tried any harder, I'd end up in the hospital.

Play the most gorgeous melody using a single finger. If you're conscientious, you'll play the same melody ten times. And if you're conscientious and creative, you'll then play ten different melodies. Your right index finger doesn't sing in the same way as your left pinky.

Play any piece in your repertory without looking at your hands. Instead, look at an imaginary camera to your right and, while playing, tell stories and jokes out loud to the audience of your TV show. Or, if you prefer, describe the piece you're playing. Like everything else, it takes practice.

Make loose fists with both hands, and play an improvisation of gentle sounds. How long can you improvise under a constraint before becoming bored or annoyed? There's always more to discover, more to invent, more to conquer.

You've seen online video clips of a dog at the piano, standing on its hind legs and playing notes with its front paws. And the dog, of course, sings and howls at the same time. The absence of judgment and censorship makes some dogs authentically musical. Yes, I suggest you play random notes as a dog would, and that you sing and howl at the same time.

Some of these constraints appear to be dumb jokes and a waste of time. And yet, practicing to a constraint *always* invites creativity and adaptability. They improve the workings of your brain, which isn't a joke nor a waste of time. In addition, accessing your creative resources sometimes requires a lowering of intellectual barriers. Silliness relaxes the mind, and the relaxed mind can be surprisingly fertile.

Let's say it again: every musical constraint is a physical constraint, and vice versa. The musical dimensions of example 6.13 are obvious: time signature, key signature, intervals. Its physical dimensions follow closely: left hand only, every note played by the little finger.

EXAMPLE 6.13 A constraint

The snippet in example 6.13 is a celebrated musical archetype with a compelling rhetorical power, part of a great compositional tradition that consists in improvising variations upon a fixed, repeated bass line. Example 6.14 shows one possible outcome. I'll title it "Obsedanta," which is Esperanto for *obsessive*. You can play it as is, or tweak and vary it, or transpose it, or—well, you get the idea. The example is only one possibility among thousands.

▶ Video Clip 26, "Improvising to a Constraint."

EXAMPLE 6.14 "Obsedanta" ©Pedro de Alcantara

The Singing and Speaking Thumbs

In daily life, the thumbs anchor the hands and give them tremendous power. Logically, the thumbs anchor pianistic technique as well. Assign musical and expressive tasks to your thumbs, and they'll become alert and responsive—to their own benefit, and to the benefit of your overall technique.

Play scales and improvisations using nothing but the thumbs. Play any piece in your repertory giving extra attention to what your thumbs are doing at any given moment. Or construct exercises and compositions with the explicit goal of getting the thumbs to speak and sing. Example 6.15 fixes the little fingers in place and lets the thumbs roam. We'll give it the title "Thimble."

▶ Video Clip 25, "Singing Thumbs."

EXAMPLE 6.15 "Thimble" ©Pedro de Alcantara

When the left and right hands play notes and chords in close proximity, pianists usually try not to crowd one into the other, often by lifting one of the wrists relatively high in space. Here we'll purposefully bring the hands close together, softly nesting the base of one thumb in the crook of the other (figure 6.2). The result is a surprising relaxation of both hands and the production of remarkable sonorities, loud and deep, rich in overtones.

▶ Video Clip 27, "Nested Thumbs."

 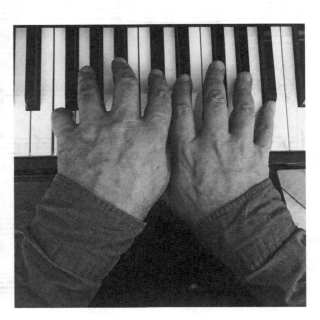

FIGURE 6.2 Nested thumbs

My theory says that the feeling of relaxed hands that you acquire through the nested thumbs stays with you after you un-nest your thumbs and return your hands to their normal positions. Example 6.16 tests the theory. Using a snippet from "Dialogue," it invites you play the same sequence twice: first with nested thumbs, then with conventional fingerings and hand positions. I'll call it a composition and title it "Empty Nest." The nesting occurs in bar six. After you strike the chord, hold it and slowly nest your hands before going on with the chord sequence. In bar 15, un-nest your hands after you strike the chord.

EXAMPLE 6.16 "Empty Nest" ©Pedro de Alcantara

Creative Health for Pianists

In the previous exercise, one thumb nested gently in the crook of the other. We'll practice a related technique. Park your right thumb on top of the left thumb. In and of itself, this is an interesting pyschomotor skill. How heavy will you make your right hand? How firm will you make your left thumb, the better to resist the right hand's weight and pressure? Is it going to be more like arm wrestling, or more like T'ai Chi? It's *always* useful to practice gradations, and it's *almost always* preferable not to use dumb force. Play a one-octave scale with the left and right thumbs in unison, the right on top of the left (example 6.17). Caress, friendship, collaboration, a light-hearted choreography. After the scale, explore the same technique in improvisations.

EXAMPLE 6.17 Stacked thumbs

Example 6.18 employs the friendship of stacked thumbs in a composition titled "Remorse." You're not obliged to stack the thumbs; it's perfectly possible to play the piece keeping a varying amount of space between the thumbs. Stacking them, however, will create a particular interpretation.

EXAMPLE 6.18 "Remorse" ©Pedro de Alcantara

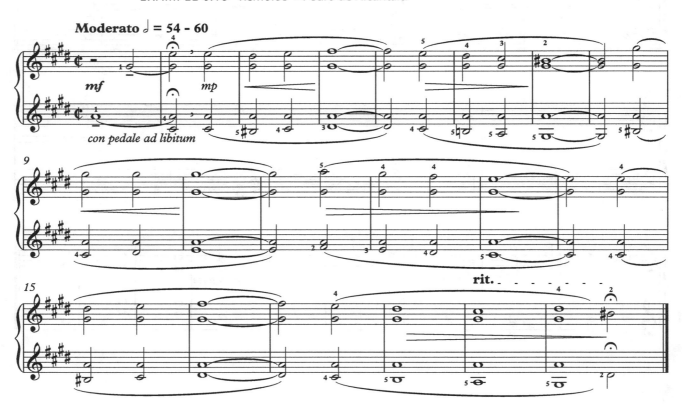

Gesture, Anatomy, and Personality

Your hands are what you think and feel about them. If you start thinking and feeling differently, the hands will change.

Suppose that you tell yourself, "I don't have a lot of stretch between these fingers. It's the way I'm built." It's possible that your hand will confirm your observation for you, behaving as if absolutely and fatally incapable of stretching. But the true capabilities of the hand (and the whole person) are partly hidden from habitual perception. Over the years, you've made a series of shifts from impossible to possible. You learned to control your sphincters, to read and write, to use a computer, to speak a foreign language—all of which were impossible before they became possible. Your voice is changeable. Posture, breathing, locomotion, sleep, digestion, taste in clothes, marriage dynamics, all of it is potentially changeable. I'm not saying that it's easy to change, only that it's possible.

Your hands, then, are changeable by birth (figure 6.3).

FIGURE 6.3 The growth of hands

The behavior of the hand (and the whole person) is partly determined by issues of "should, shouldn't," "right, wrong," "allowed, forbidden," "ugly, beautiful," "me, not me." We tend not to be fully alert to these strictures, their rules and exceptions, their potential punishments. We learned them long ago, as children. And we learned them under the threat of embarrassment and humiliation.

We'll take the example of the stretch between fingers. Your hands would become "bigger" if you relaxed them and gained some stretch between your fingers. They might become too big, people would notice them, your hands might become not proper, even bestial. "In our family we all have small hands." This can be an observation about biological features or a stricture. "If your hands aren't like ours, you don't belong with us. Big hands disgust us!" Familial and social exclusion is quite a threat, particularly to a child. Therefore, the hands will stay small; or inept, since we're a family of disembodied introverts and academics; or accident-prone, since you've always been accident-prone and Momma loves-and-hates you for being so clumsy, so don't you change now!

Caressing the keys, pressing them down, holding and releasing them, pushing and pulling; contact of skin to key; the wrists affirming themselves, the fingertips curious and adventurous . . . playing the piano is an intimate affair. The sensuality of touching the piano can trouble some people, who might not be able to explain it rationally. They'll claim that they're just awkward at the piano, when in reality their awkwardness comes from psychological issues not directly caused by the piano. Sensuality can be hard to handle, so to speak.

The passing of the thumb as you move up and down the keyboard illustrates some of these complications. If it feels wrong to release your thumb, or to gently fold it, or to adapt its shape and behavior; if you have preconceived ideas of how to do it and how you *should* do it; if you don't agree to the feeling of a flexible and independent thumb, you won't render your thumb flexible and independent. You won't be able to solve this problem physically, because it isn't a physical problem to begin with. You'll need to learn the aesthetics of adaptable hands, the sounds and the musicality of free thumbs, the personality and the emotions of this touch.

Example 6.19 is an exercise and a meditation. How tenderly, how sweetly, how lovingly will you play every note, and also every silence?

EXAMPLE 6.19 Adaptability

If you'd like to explore this principle in exercises and improvisations, encapsulate it in this way: three-note chords, the middle note played by the thumb. There are dozens of such chords, and uncountable ways of stringing them in musically interesting sequences.

Example 6.20 is a short composition inspired by the principle we've just studied. I think it's faintly reminiscent of some of Béla Bartók's work in his marvelous *Mikrokosmos*, and I'll title it "Mikro" as a modest homage to the great man.

EXAMPLE 6.20 "Mikro"

Example 6.21 is a little more demanding. Let's call it "Love Left."

EXAMPLE 6.21 "Love Left" ©Pedro de Alcantara

Creative Health for Pianists

Example 6.22 increases the demands on your left hand. We'll title it "Envelope," referring to the fingers and palm gently enveloping the thumb in their soft embrace. At first, take it a measure at a time, playing slowly and using fermatas to relax your mind and your hand. I like keeping the same fingering for all chords, but you could potentially hurt yourself depending on how your hands are built and how you employ them. Decide how often you'll use the enveloped fingering (with the thumb playing and holding the first note of every bar) and when you'll finger it differently for the convenience of your hand or for interpretative reasons.

EXAMPLE 6.22 "Envelope" ©Pedro de Alcantara

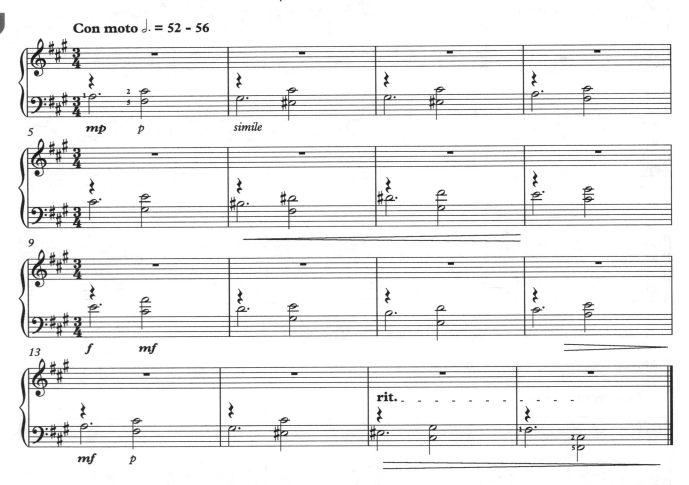

Example 6.23 demands a sensitive and expressive right hand, belonging to a sensitive and expressive musician. We'll title it "Love Right." My score proposes a combination of enveloped and un-enveloped fingerings.

EXAMPLE 6.23 "Love Right" ©Pedro de Alcantara

ADVANCED SEESAW 7

Compositions
- The Party (example 7.1)
- Cloverleaf (example 7.7)
- Piper (example 7.8)
- Cloverleaf Piper (example 7.9)
- The Twelve (example 7.11)
- Aloysia (example 7.12)
- Constanze (example 7.14)
- Aloysia's Travels (example 7.18)
- Aloysia's Accidental Travels (example 7.19)
- Seesaw of Heartbreak (example 7.22)
- Odd Man Blues (example 7.24)
- Catch the Breeze (example 7.26)
- Breezy (example 7.27)

Video Clips
- 28. The Party
- 29. Cloverleaf
- 30. Aloysia
- 31. Left Aloysia
- 32. Seesaw of Heartbreak
- 33. Odd Man Blues
- 34. Catch the Breeze

In chapter 3 we practiced the seesaw principle of up-and-down finger movements using a specific rhythmic pattern in $\frac{12}{8}$. Here we continue exploring the principle, using new rhythmic and fingering patterns of increasing complexity.

First, I'll show you a composition—or, more precisely, a suggested composition among a thousand possibilities (example 7.1). Then, we'll take the composition apart after you play it—or, more precisely, after you play *with* it. It's called "The Party."

▶ Video Clip 28, "The Party."

Advanced Seesaw

EXAMPLE 7.1 "The Party" ©Pedro de Alcantara

The intervals and fingerings allow your hands to assume a relaxed position without stretches. Accents and articulations, the alternation of short and long notes, and the placement of rests invite your hands to use the keyboard as a sort of trampoline.

The initial chord is C major with an added seventh. Is it a beautiful little thing, or an annoying little thing? If you find it annoying, you probably need a vacation. Let the exercise itself be the vacation. Suspend judgment, organize your hands, and start bouncing up and down the keyboard at a speed of your liking. The composer wrote a series of parallel fifths as if he wasn't aware that grownups don't "do" parallel fifths. But you're on vacation and you don't have to be a grownup (figure 7.1).

FIGURE 7.1 Hands at the party

One way of thinking about the seesaw mechanism is to compare its up-and-down motions with takeoffs and landings. Example 7.2 illustrates the idea. In the first bar, the first chord represents a landing and the second, a takeoff. Why add a fermata to the takeoff chord, and why make it loud? It's an invitation to connect with the ground, the better to jump and fly. "Up" and "down" are enmeshed. They work together; one contains the other; one is the other.

EXAMPLE 7.2 Takeoff and landing

"The Party" is built on rhythmic patterns with articulations, inflections, and dynamics. Example 7.3 catalogs these patterns. Choose how long you want to use a pattern before changing to a different one, and how long you want to linger on a chord before transposing it up or down the keyboard.

Creative Health for Pianists

EXAMPLE 7.3 A catalog of patterns

Now retain the chords and their fingerings, but start altering the rhythms and articulations (example 7.4). A big accent such as a loud sforzando is like an explosion. Who explodes? Not the pianist, but the sound itself. You'll produce a better sonic explosion by keeping yourself relatively still and in an upright posture.

EXAMPLE 7.4 Rhythms, articulations, accents

Creative Health for Pianists

Cloverleaf and Piper

The next exercise-composition assigns the seesaw mechanism to the left hand (example 7.5). For now, we're back in E Major, a tonality that's friendly to your pianistic hand. The intervals are an interesting conflict between consonance and dissonance. The gesture's rhythms invite contact and release. Fingers go up and down in response.

EXAMPLE 7.5 Bouncy left hand

Put the gesture on a loop and vary its inflections and dynamics (example 7.6). Use fine gradations from *pp* to *ff* and from staccatissimo to legatissimo, together with accents and stresses.

EXAMPLE 7.6 Inflections and gradations

Add a right-hand melody to the left-hand pattern (example 7.7). Make up your own melody, or use the one I propose, which requires hand crossing. I call this composition "Cloverleaf."

▶ Video Clip 29, "Cloverleaf."

EXAMPLE 7.7 "Cloverleaf" ©Pedro de Alcantara

At the piano and away from it, the left and right sides of your body are in constant dialogue. The dialogue can be a shouting match, when one side seems to be in conflict with the other; or a collaboration, when one side offers reassurance and stability to the other. We'll name this dialogue *bilateral transfer*—that is, the transfer of information and sensation from side to side. Collaboration or fight, bilateral transfer never stops. If your left-hand seesaw is comfortable and reliable, it'll help the right hand find its own comfort. And vice versa.

How many different melodies can you add to the left-hand pattern? If you include every type of melody in your calculations—the crazy, the ugly, the illegal, the diabolical—then the number is in the billions. If you decide that your melody has to behave, then the number is in the thousands only, or in the hundreds, or in the dozens. It doesn't matter; what matters is that you can fit quite a lot of different melodies over the same bass line. Sit at the piano, play the bass line on a loop, and spend the afternoon discovering some of those melodies.

Let's look at another melody, which I call "Piper" (example 7.8). It's in the Mixolydian mode, about which we'll learn more in chapter 9. If you feel threatened by the word "Mixolydian," say to yourself that the melody is in E major with a flat seventh—that is, a D natural. This is a theoretical approximation; it isn't exactly right to call the Mixolydian mode a major scale with a flat seventh. But for now your two main choices are to worry or to not worry.

Creative Health for Pianists

EXAMPLE 7.8 "Piper" ©Pedro de Alcantara

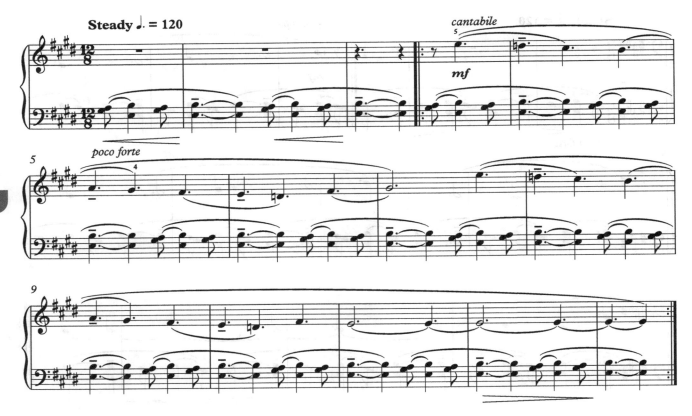

Play the two melodies in sequence, going back to the first melody after playing the second one. This creates an ABA structure—or, more precisely, AABBA if we take the repeats into consideration. The composition doesn't go anywhere harmonically. Does this matter? No. Bagpipes don't go anywhere harmonically either. India's Carnatic music also ignores harmony. We're in good company. We'll call this composition "Cloverleaf Piper" (example 7.9).

Consider the composition as the background to a choreography with two characters. A man and a woman? A man and a boy? Father and son, father and daughter, two sisters? You're the composer. You decide.

Advanced Seesaw

EXAMPLE 7.9 "Cloverleaf Piper" ©Pedro de Alcantara

The Twelve

Our "Cloverleaf" and "Piper" explorations were born of a simple but stimulating left-hand pattern. It feels good to practice it slow or fast, legato or staccato. It feels good to add right-hand melodies to it. And it also feels good to transpose the pattern to different keys.

How about we transpose the pattern to all twelve keys, moving counterclockwise along the circle of fifths? Example 7.10 lays the sequence out. The fingering never changes. Put the metronome on and ride the horse round and round. Do you find it hard to place the sharps and flats? Slow the horse down.

Advanced Seesaw

EXAMPLE 7.10 Bouncy pattern around the circle

Now, how about we compose different melodies for each key? How about we cross hands for some of the melodies? And how about we alternate major keys and the Mixolydian mode? My version of this challenge is called "The Twelve" (example 7.11).

Creative Health for Pianists

Isolate a section and practice it as a self-contained unit. Loop, tweak, rearrange. On purpose I didn't add many dynamic and inflection markings. The blank slate is yours to color.

EXAMPLE 7.11 "The Twelve" ©Pedro de Alcantara

EXAMPLE 7.11 Continued

Creative Health for Pianists

EXAMPLE 7.11 Continued

Advanced Seesaw

EXAMPLE 7.11 Continued

Creative Health for Pianists

EXAMPLE 7.11 Continued

EXAMPLE 7.11 Continued

EXAMPLE 7.11 Continued

Aloysia

This is a gesture for the right hand. Its name refers to the singer Aloysia Weber (1760–1839), who was Mozart's sister-in-law. I begin by showing you an elaborate version, partly to invite you to keep your cool when confronted with something that looks too difficult (example 7.12).

Video Clip 30, "Aloysia."

EXAMPLE 7.12 "Aloysia" ©Pedro de Alcantara

The gesture is asymmetrical. Some fingers are close to one another, others are spread out. The time signature, the rhythms, and the articulations seem complicated. A demon whispers into your ears: "Play it fast and perfect, or you aren't any good."

What to do?

Disobey the demon. You don't have to play it fast and perfect. You don't have to play it at all! Choose to play or not to play, to play fast or to play slow, to play loud or to play soft, to play it as written or to rewrite it.

Rewriting is one of the most helpful techniques for every musician. Reduce the gesture down to its most basic element: a C-major scale. Example 7.13 lays out the journey from the scale to the elaborate gesture. It goes like this:

1. Start with a C-major scale.
2. Add first-inversion chords.
3. Add sevenths.
4. Split each four-note chord into two two-note chords.
5. Shorten the second of the two chords.
6. Add a lilting rhythm.

Advanced Seesaw

EXAMPLE 7.13 Deconstruction

Example 7.14 encapsulates the previous process. Play the piano part and hum, sing, or whistle the scale at the same time. How fast, how slow, how percussive, how lyrical? You

decide. Dynamics, inflections, accents, pedal? You decide. Is this an exercise or a composition? I decide: it's a composition. We'll call it "Constanze," who was Aloysia's sister and Mozart's wife.

EXAMPLE 7.14 "Constanze" ©Pedro de Alcantara

Example 7.15 shows the simplified version of the simplified version. I could have started this section with the simplest version—as I have with other exercises in the book. But there's merit in alternating between going from simple to complex, and going from complex to simple. Play those few bars on a repeating loop. Organize your hand and fingers in the intriguing shape required by the intriguing intervals. Land, take off, land, take off: accents and inflections make the takeoff and landing easier.

EXAMPLE 7.15 Simplification

We're ready for variations: easy, less easy, right hand alone, right hand over a left-hand drone, right hand with an impossibly high melody played by the left hand crossing over the right (example 7.16). Plus all the variations you'll invent yourself.

Creative Health for Pianists

EXAMPLE 7.16 Varying "Aloysia"

It's tempting to focus on the physical dimensions of the seesaw mechanism: fingers and fingerings, hand shapes, the behavior of the wrist and arm. These are important, but a comfortable seesaw ride isn't a physical affair but a musical one. Example 7.17 compares three slightly different variations.

EXAMPLE 7.17 Note groupings

The time signature, rhythms, notes, and fingerings don't vary. Articulations and inflections, which create distinct note groupings, do vary. Play each of these variations slowly. Then play them at a faster tempo without neglecting these interpretive decisions, which are also physical decisions. I think you'll find the third version the easiest to play, on account of its musical logic.

We've been dwelling in the world of C major, or what we often call "white keys." But nothing prevents us from transposing "Aloysia" to any other key. I've laid out a counterclockwise path along the circle of fifths, transposing it down a perfect fifth again and again until I arrive back at the starting point of C major (example 7.18). I call this sequence "Aloysia's Travels." It's a festival of black and white keys in multiple combinations, asking your fingers to adapt to numerous positions, some of them quite demanding.

"Aloysia" boils down to a diatonic major scale. If her travels threaten you, isolate one of the keys—it's only four bars long. Then isolate the scale for the key you chose—it's only eight notes long. Embellish it calmly and sweetly, interval by interval, bar by bar, and finally key by key. You won't be the first person to fall in love with Aloysia.

I've also laid out the travels without key-signature changes (example 7.19). This allows you to follow, visually and graphically, the path of flats and sharps Aloysia takes from beginning to end. Which one do you prefer, the first version with key-signature changes (where the accidentals are seemingly hidden) or the second version (which is full of in-your-face accidentals)? It's the same piece, but they look so different! Let's give this oh-so-different version a new title: "Aloysia's Accidental Travels."

Creative Health for Pianists

EXAMPLE 7.18 "Aloysia's Travels" ©Pedro de Alcantara

Advanced Seesaw

EXAMPLE 7.18 Continued

Creative Health for Pianists

EXAMPLE 7.19 "Aloysia's Accidental Travels" ©Pedro de Alcantara

Advanced Seesaw

EXAMPLE 7.19 Continued

The Left-hand Seesaw Series

We'll study four similar seesaw patterns employing the left hand. Example 7.20 shows the patterns in their minimal or archetypal forms. You can see how they use the same starting point: a C-major chord in first inversion (which, as you may have noticed, is also behind other ideas in this book). I've laid out the starting point, the notes added to the chord, and the rhythmic formulas we'll use in our explorations.

EXAMPLE 7.20 The left-hand seesaw series

Left Aloysia

"Aloysia" can be easily transposed to the left hand, although its physicality is challenging on account of the stretch between little and ring fingers. If you try to muscle through the stretch, you're likely to hurt yourself. But if you spend time finding nuances of voicing and timing, it's possible that the stretch will become softer in your hand. Example 7.21 shows you a series of voicing explorations using rhythm and dynamics. Use these explorations as an entry point into improvisation and composition.

Video Clip 31, "Left Aloysia."

Advanced Seesaw

EXAMPLE 7.21 Workout for "Left Aloysia"

EXAMPLE 7.21 Continued

Seesaw of Heartbreak

Example 7.22 shows you a series of building blocks for an improvisational and compositional game. At the end of the example I lay out the beginning of a composition, which I title "Seesaw of Heartbreak." Your job is to put together your own sequences, your own improvised compositions.

Below is a descriptive list of the building blocks. You don't have to read the list; if you prefer, just play through example 7.22 a few times, until you sense how the game is constructed.

1. Play a left-hand seesaw of thumb and index finger.
2. Articulate and inflect the seesaw mechanism.
3. Take the seesaw up and down the keyboard, creating an embellished C-major scale.
4. Add a bass line played by the little finger.
5. Remind yourself of the intervals from "Heartbreak."
6. Bring together the left-hand seesaw and the intervals from "Heartbreak."
7. Practice right-hand speeds. Start by holding the right-hand interval over a whole bar.
8. Play a dotted half followed by a dotted quarter.
9. Play three dotted quarters.
10. Play an asymmetrical count with a displaced accent.
11. Add melodic motion.
12. Mix and match.

Video Clip 32, "Seesaw of Heartbreak."

Creative Health for Pianists

EXAMPLE 7.22 "Seesaw of Heartbreak" ©Pedro de Alcantara

EXAMPLE 7.22 Continued

12 Seesaw of Heartbreak
Allegro con moto ♩. = 126

Odd Man Blues

I took a couple of two-note chords, strung them in a sequence, and added a melodic possibility (example 7.23).

▶ Video Clip 33, "Odd Man Blues."

EXAMPLE 7.23 An introduction to "Odd Man Blues"

Using these basic materials, I created a musical structure where each section has three phrases of five bars each (hence the title "Odd Man Blues"). In example 7.24 I lay out how I like performing it, starting with the left hand alone and adding melodic and rhythmic layers one by one. Watch out for the time-signature and tempo change toward the end.

Advanced Seesaw

EXAMPLE 7.24 "Odd Man Blues" ©Pedro de Alcantara

Creative Health for Pianists

EXAMPLE 7.24 Continued

EXAMPLE 7.24 Continued

Catch the Breeze

Depending on your hand's size and shape, the left-hand seesaw of "Catch the Breeze" might hurt you if you try to hold the pattern's four notes in a single position. Example 7.25 is a preparatory step that invites you to conceive of the pattern as two separate groups of two notes, with space and release between them. When the time comes for you to play the composition itself (example 7.26), you'll know to keep the left-hand pattern breezy and light.

▶ Video Clip 34, "Catch the Breeze."

EXAMPLE 7.25 An introduction to "Catch the Breeze"

Creative Health for Pianists

EXAMPLE 7.26 "Catch the Breeze" ©Pedro de Alcantara

Advanced Seesaw

EXAMPLE 7.26 Continued

Do you find "Catch the Breeze" intimidating, in rhythms and finger work? I created a skeletal version with a couple of melodic adjustments. I titled it "Breezy" (example 7.27). You could skip the elaborate version and concentrate on the easy one, or play the easy one first and immediately follow it with the elaborate one.

EXAMPLE 7.27 "Breezy" ©Pedro de Alcantara

Advanced Seesaw

EXAMPLE 7.27 Continued

SONIC PLAY 8

Compositions

- Primus (example 8.3)
- Secundus (example 8.4)
- Tertius (example 8.5)
- Quartus (example 8.6)
- Quintus (example 8.7)
- Sextus (example 8.8)
- Septimus (example 8.9)
- Octavus (example 8.10)
- Nonus (example 8.11)
- Skend (example 8.12)
- Serpentipedi (example 8.13)
- Iocus (example 8.14)
- Octaviana (example 8.15)
- Quest (example 8.16)
- Composure (example 8.18)
- I Love Albers (example 8.23)
- Chroma (example 8.24)
- Sharp Neighbor (example 8.25)
- Minor Albers (example 8.26)
- The Albers Sequence (example 8.27)
- Rising Light (example 8.31)
- Yale Key (example 8.32)
- Waltz for Anni (example 8.33)
- Zwölf (example 8.34)
- Crossed Albers (example 8.35)

Video Clips

35. Intertwining
36. Albers
37. The Albers Sequence
38. Transpositions by Thirds
39. Smooth Transpositions

Creative Health for Pianists. Pedro de Alcantara, Oxford University Press. © Oxford University Press 2023.
DOI: 10.1093/oso/9780197600207.003.0009

Our starting point or archetype is a two-bar pattern suggesting a *moto perpetuo* (example 8.1). The first bar in the example is there only to show that the pattern is derived from our friend "Dialogue" from chapter 1.

EXAMPLE 8.1 The intertwining archetype

The outer voices are comparatively slow and stable, the inner voices fast and dynamic. Little fingers get to sing the melody and bass, inner fingers add consonance, dissonance, and rhythmic drive. Fingers, notes, sounds, and rhythms are intertwined, as they always are in music; but our archetype condenses and magnetizes the principle. Get the hang of it, and other manifestations of intertwining become easier to play—including those in the mainstream repertory.

Put it on a loop. Try different tempi and dynamics. Get your little fingers to highlight the outer notes, then get your thumbs to highlight the inner voices. Offbeat accents would be lovely. Add a fermata here and there. In its basic form, "Intertwining" isn't hard to play. It means you could use it as a warm-up tool, and also as a meditation. Is something making you anxious or distracted? Sit at the piano and spin "Intertwining" for a few minutes.

Video Clip 35, "Intertwining."

Varied, stretched, and transposed, "Intertwining" lends itself to a game. It's like playing with Lego and building something original by combining assorted bricks. We'll employ eight sound bricks. Stay with the white keys, keeping your improvisation-composition diatonic in C major. Or transpose it to any other key if you like. Choose which bricks to use and for how long. Choose to keep the bricks where they are, or to move them by seconds up or down the keyboard.

Example 8.2 shows the bricks, cataloged in a stripped-down version. Underneath the catalog, there's a brief reminder of the rhythmic construction of "Intertwining."

EXAMPLE 8.2 The intertwining catalog

Here is each brick, described and illustrated. The rules of the game allow you to add pattern-breaking musical endings to a sequence. Simple compositions are often enhanced by clever titles. I'll use the Latin ordinal names for this series.

1. The two-bar germinating seed, unchanged (example 8.3). Use it once, or repeat it as many times as you wish. "Primus."

EXAMPLE 8.3 "Primus" ©Pedro de Alcantara

2. Transpose the second bar of the germinating seed up or down, then transpose this new unit up or down (example 8.4). "Secundus."

EXAMPLE 8.4 "Secundus" ©Pedro de Alcantara

3. Take the first quarter note of the germinating seed as an autonomous element, then transpose it up or down (example 8.5). "Tertius."

EXAMPLE 8.5 "Tertius" ©Pedro de Alcantara

4. Use two quarter-note units with changing pitches, then transpose an entire bar up or down (example 8.6). Notice that the first quarter of the bar is the same pitch as the second quarter of the preceding bar. "Quartus."

EXAMPLE 8.6 "Quartus" ©Pedro de Alcantara

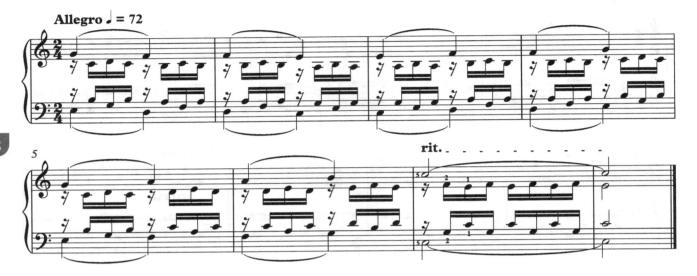

5. Use two quarter notes with changing pitches, followed by a half note with the same pitch as the second of the previous quarter notes (example 8.7). "Quintus." It's nice playing it an octave lower, at a moderate speed.

EXAMPLE 8.7 "Quintus" ©Pedro de Alcantara

6. Use two quarter notes with unchanging pitches, followed by a half note plus a quarter note with a pitch change (example 8.8). "Sextus."

EXAMPLE 8.8 "Sextus" ©Pedro de Alcantara

Creative Health for Pianists

7. Use a quarter-note upbeat, followed by a half note plus a quarter note with a pitch change (example 8.9). "Septimus."

EXAMPLE 8.9 "Septimus" ©Pedro de Alcantara

8. Use two quarter notes plus a half note, with unidirectional changing pitches (example 8.10). "Octavus."

EXAMPLE 8.10 "Octavus" ©Pedro de Alcantara

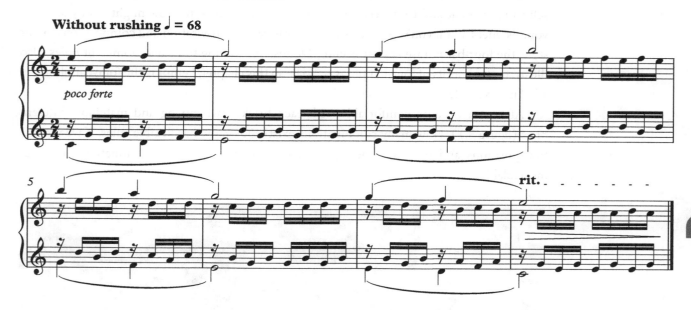

Mix and Match

When you play with bricks, you can build a shapeless thing or a solid structure according to a plan. Both have their merits. Similarly, our game of improvisation allows you to put any two bricks together and create something small and forgettable, or to design a composition with coherent phrase lengths, varied melodic directions, and some staying power in your listeners' hearts.

Two tools increase compositional coherence. Among the chords of "Intertwining," one is close to a tonic chord, despite being a bit ambiguous in its sounds; and another is a dominant-seventh chord in first inversion (example 8.11). Both chords are handy phrase poles, convenient as departing points or arrival destinations. "Nonus."

EXAMPLE 8.11 "Nonus" ©Pedro de Alcantara

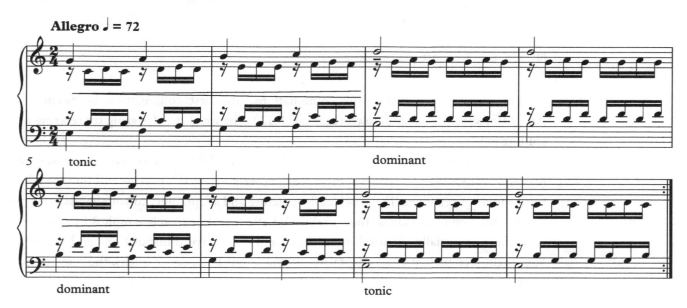

Creative Health for Pianists

The traditional four-bar phrase length is memorable. Easy to comprehend, it lends itself to movement and to dance. Too many four-bar phrases in a row might annoy some of your listeners, but if you're looking to create coherent improvisation and compositions in our style, the four-bar phrase is your friend. "Nonus," illustrating tonic and dominant poles, also illustrates the merits of four-bar phrases. So far in this chapter, I employ the four-bar phrase in all of my examples except for "Sextus."

After you become comfortable with each brick, start mixing and matching different ones (figure 8.1). How many combinations exist? Our game has flexible rules. If we include transpositions and tweaks in our game, the number of possible combinations becomes incalculable.

FIGURE 8.1 Architect and composer

I'm showing you five of my combinations. The first combination is "Skend," a straightforward trip up and down (example 8.12). The word *skend* is slang for relaxing or chilling out.

The second combination is "Serpentipedi," which is Latin for serpentine or snake-like (example 8.13). It starts with a sort of crawling walk where the pinkies and thumbs take turns moving in tandem. The crawl lends structure and adaptability to your hands.

The third combination is "Iocus," which is Latin for joke or jest (example 8.14). "Iocus" is in three essentially identical sections, except for octave transpositions and accents. You might recognize it as an adaptation of one of our basic sonic bricks, the one named "Octavus."

To help you understand the workings of the compositional game, and also to help you play "Iocus" more comfortably, I put together a sort of practice sequence: "Octavus," followed by a pinkie-thumb crawl similar to "Serpentipedi," followed by a segment of "Iocus." I'm calling this sequence "Octaviana" (example 8.15).

"Quest," my last combination, merits a few remarks. I took the mix-and-match game further than before by alternating building blocks from "Intertwining," "Dialogue," and "Heartbreak." Within the modest compositional ambitions of our game, this structure is varied and coherent (8.16). I invite you to employ its principle in your own mixing-and-matching.

EXAMPLE 8.12 "Skend" ©Pedro de Alcantara

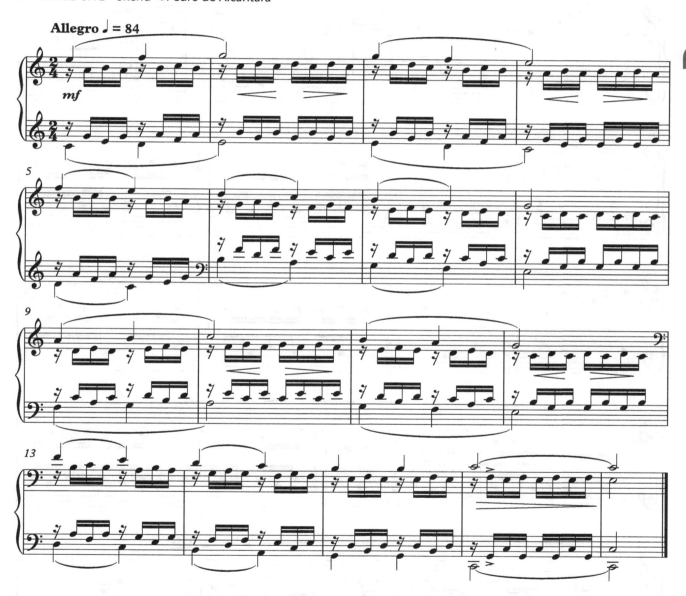

EXAMPLE 8.13 "Serpentipedi" ©Pedro de Alcantara

EXAMPLE 8.14 "locus" ©Pedro de Alcantara

EXAMPLE 8.15 "Octaviana" ©Pedro de Alcantara

EXAMPLE 8.16 "Quest" ©Pedro de Alcantara

Creative Health for Pianists

EXAMPLE 8.16 Continued

Transposition

In chapter 5 we started practicing the art of transposition. So far in this chapter, every example has been diatonic in C major. But there's no reason why you wouldn't transpose any or all of it to a different key. To illustrate the point, we'll approach the key of A♭ major, partly because it sounds good and partly because it requires a marvelous combination of black and white keys. By now you've memorized the fingerings for the archetype. They apply to this version, too.

I've laid out two exercises or compositional variations. Example 8.17 is a sequence of accelerating complications. Notice the occasional fermata over a bar line: it's an invitation to stop and think through the notes and fingerings you need to play on the next bar. Example 8.18 is reassuringly steady. I'll give it a title: "Composure."

EXAMPLE 8.17 Intertwining transposition

EXAMPLE 8.18 "Composure" ©Pedro de Alcantara

Albers

A cousin of "Intertwining" introduces new sonic and improvisational possibilities. Example 8.19 shows the pattern in its archetypal form, which I call "Albers." Josef Albers (1888–1976) was a great visual artist who, among many accomplishments, studied and mastered the juxtaposition of colors. Soon we'll be transposing "Albers" up and down the keyboard, creating tonal and coloristic juxtapositions.

EXAMPLE 8.19 "Albers"

"Albers" is rhythmically identical to "Intertwining," but different in intervals. Various notes vibrate in sympathy one with the other (example 8.20). Becoming alert to these vibrations will change the way you play and increase your enjoyment of sounds and sonic relationships. Work with the right pedal, without it; linger on this or that note; try variations of dynamics, timing, and touch. Sympathetic vibration is a deep and detailed art; here we only scratch its surface. The example includes the first eight harmonics for the fundamental C, because it's the harmonic series that determines sympathetic vibrations.

▶ Video Clip 36, "Albers."

EXAMPLE 8.20 Sympathetic vibrations

"Albers" is musically ambiguous. In its basic form, it isn't unequivocally in C major, but in our minds' ears we tend to make it be in C major. As we spin the pattern, we may resolve it explicitly in C major, meeting our expectations; or in C minor, confounding and delighting our expectations. Or we might never resolve it (example 8.21).

EXAMPLE 8.21 Unresolved ambiguity

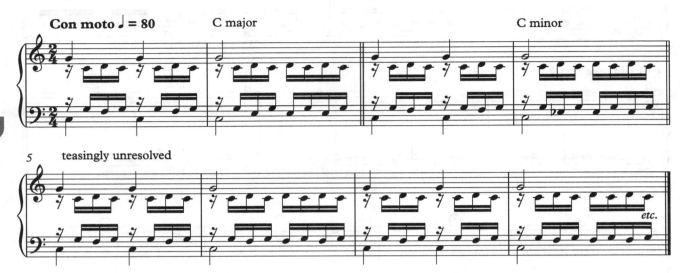

Part of our work with "Albers" consists in transposing it. The intervals and fingerings don't change when you transpose it. Suppose you find the version in C comfortable. All you need is to find the notes and the black or white keys you need to play it in F, for instance, and it'll be just as comfortable.

In example 8.22 I lay out the start of the C, F, and B♭ versions. Keep going counterclockwise around the circle of fifths. Or play the transpositions in chromatic order: C, D♭, D, E . . . Or use random combinations. The main thing is for you to practice in twelve keys and become comfortable in all of them.

EXAMPLE 8.22 Albers transpositions

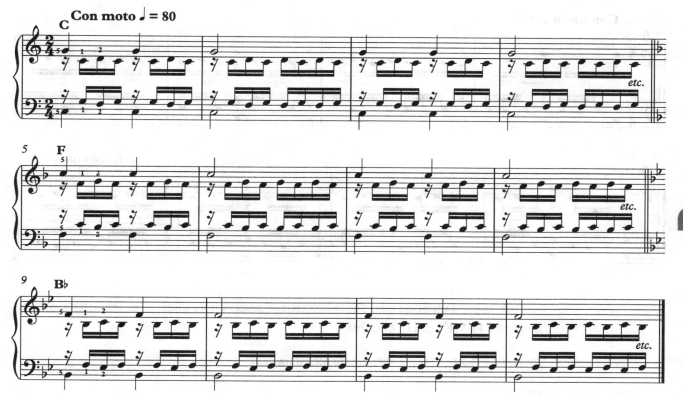

Variations

"Albers" is easy to modify. I propose four variations, which will become our Lego-like sonic bricks to improvise and compose with. One archetype plus four variations transposable to twelve keys, sixty bricks all counted. Tweaks and stretches will take the game very far.

The first variation introduces a small but significant change to the bass line (example 8.23). What we used to hear as being tonal (ambiguously in C major or C minor) suddenly reveals itself to be modal (Mixolydian). We'll call it "I Love Albers."

Creative Health for Pianists

EXAMPLE 8.23 "I Love Albers" ©Pedro de Alcantara

The second variation introduces a pattern of descending minor thirds in the left hand (example 8.24). We'll call it "Chroma."

EXAMPLE 8.24 "Chroma" ©Pedro de Alcantara

The third variation is a chromatic embellishment in the left hand, resolving the pattern first to major, then to minor (example 8.25). We'll call it "Sharp Neighbor."

EXAMPLE 8.25 "Sharp Neighbor" ©Pedro de Alcantara

The fourth variation is more elaborate (example 8.26). It's in the minor key, with movement in the bass line and a dominant-to-tonic cadence at the end. We'll call it "Minor Albers." If you've been diligently transposing the simpler variations, you'll be well prepared to tackle this slightly more complicated one.

EXAMPLE 8.26 "Minor Albers" ©Pedro de Alcantara

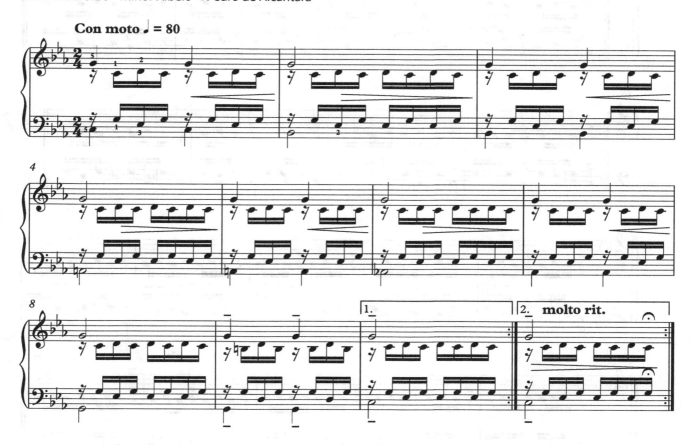

Let's compile all the Albers variations (example 8.27). You'll pass through a changing sonic territory, sometimes clearly defined as being in C major or C minor, sometimes modal rather than tonal. I'm calling this compilation "The Albers Sequence."

▶ Video Clip 37, "The Albers Sequence."

EXAMPLE 8.27 "The Albers Sequence" ©Pedro de Alcantara

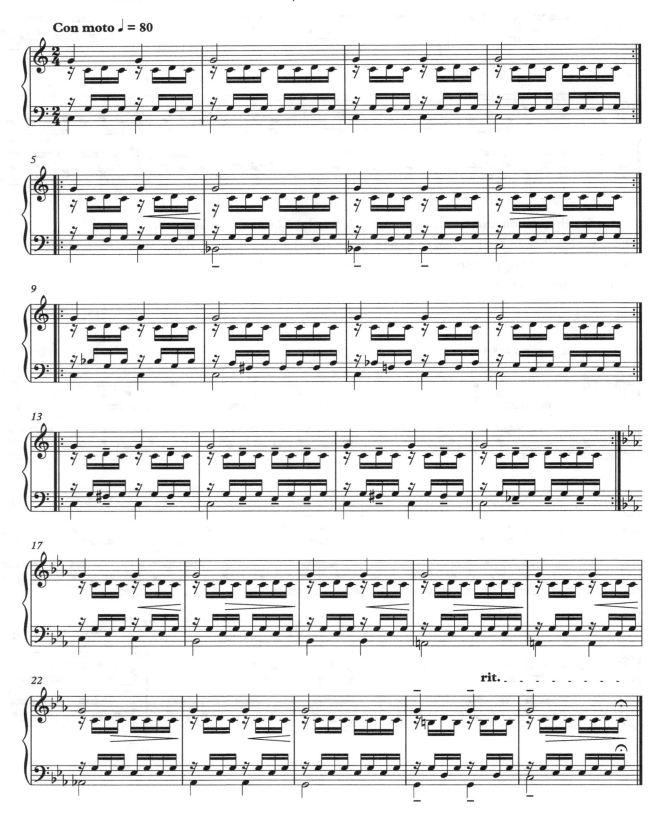

Transpositions by Thirds

"Albers" and its variations lend themselves to transpositions up by a minor third or down by a major third. For instance, if you find yourself in C minor (or in any of the chords that ends an Albers variation in C) you can move up a minor third to E♭, or down a major third to A♭ (example 8.28).

EXAMPLE 8.28 Transpositions by thirds

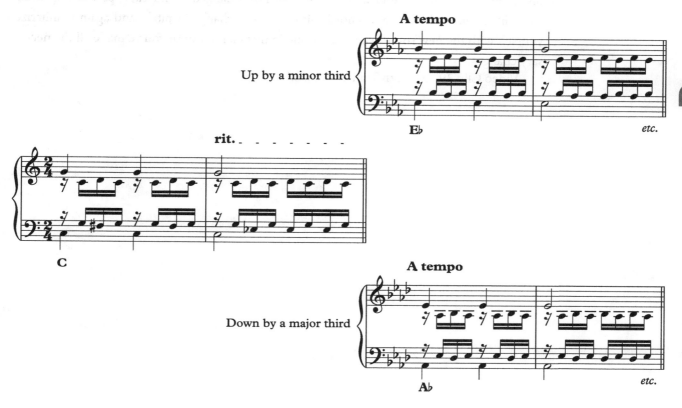

Once you arrive at your new key, you can spin things out and play variations in your new key; or go quickly to another new key. The possible combinations of transpositions and variations are limitless. You'll be forever mixing white keys and black keys. Flats and sharps could quickly start to intimidate you. But keep two things in mind:

1. Fingerings and intervals are the same in every tonality.
2. In every tonality both hands lay out perfect fifths between the thumb and the little finger.

It means that "Albers" offers you an element ease and predictability as you move into seemingly complicated tonalities.

In video clip 38 I perform a sequence of transpositions by thirds. I start in C and go up by minor thirds: E♭, F♯ (which is enharmonically equivalent to G♭), A, and arriving back at C. Then I go down by major thirds: C, A♭ (which is enharmonically equivalent to G♯), E, and C. I end with a little Mixolydian embellishment.

Video Clip 38, "Transpositions by Third."

I laid out an exercise to help you navigate your transpositions (example 8.29). To illustrate it, I chose the passage from C minor to E♭. Pause on a comfortable C-minor chord, then make one change in pitch. To familiarize yourself with the changed soundscape, play or improvise some little thing with the new chord. Make another change in pitch, and again familiarize yourself with the new soundscape. Continue in this manner until you've made all the necessary changes.

Video Clip 39, "Smooth Transpositions."

EXAMPLE 8.29 Smooth transpositions

Enharmonic Transposition

In piano playing, a G♭ and an F♯ are played on the same key and produce the same sound. As we saw in chapter 5, G♭ and F♯ are said to be *enharmonically equivalent*. C♭ and B are also enharmonically equivalent. Much like identical twins who lead separate lives with divergent destinies, enharmonically equivalent notes are identical in sound (when played at the piano) but have divergent destinies. The world of sharps offers different adventures from the world of flats.

Suppose that you're practicing the pattern in E♭, and you decide to transpose it as usual. Up by a minor third, you go from E♭ to G♭; down a major third, you go from E♭ or C♭. Both these new keys have their enharmonic equivalents: G♭ can become F♯, and C♭ can become B (example 8.30).

EXAMPLE 8.30 Enharmonic transpositions

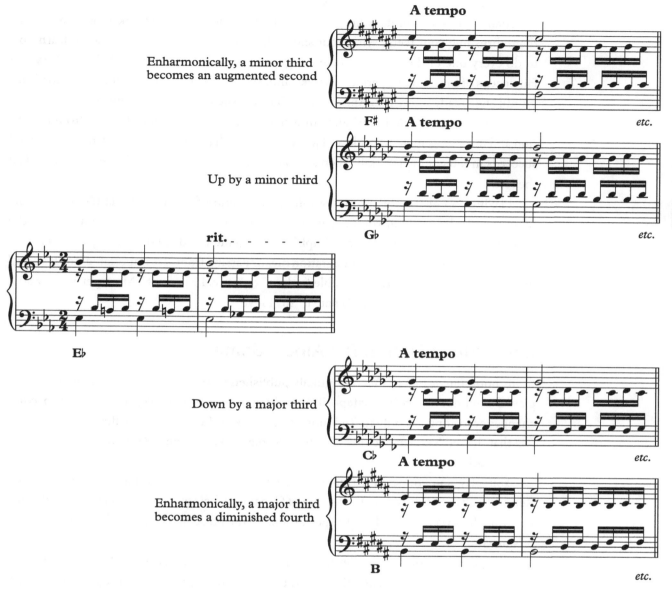

On paper, example 8.30 may look terrifying. And yet, fingerings and intervals are the same in all keys; and your hands remain comfortably framed by a perfect fifth played by thumb and little finger. Trust your hands and ears, and you might modulate up and down not by calculating flats and sharps but by bodily and aural sensations.

Like many other exercises, "Albers" is both a problem and a solution. It's a problem because it presents musical and psychophysical challenges. And it's a solution because it offers a predictable, reliable, and beautiful formula for exploring key relationships and modulations. "Albers" shows you how to shape your hands and fingers according to intervallic relationships, how to move up and down the keyboard, how to enhance sympathetic resonances through touch and timing, how to modulate by thirds (which happens to be a favorite device of Beethoven's, for instance), and how to acquaint yourself with twenty-four tonalities at the piano (twelve major keys, twelve minor keys, not counting enharmonically equivalent tonalities).

Many things in your daily life are so easy that you don't have to think about how you do them: brushing your teeth, tying your shoes, driving your car. But you've had to learn how to do every one of those things. Take tying shoes as an example. The little kid will try and fail dozens of times over a period of weeks until she can tie her shoes reliably. She can't learn it until she's ready to learn it. And when she's ready, she'll learn by an informal combination of imitating, thinking, and sensing, with many emotions thrown into the mix, from frustration and discouragement to pride and joy. Given enough practice and perseverance, the child succeeds in integrating the skill. Then she can learn advanced calculus, brain surgery, and all the rest.

Playing an enharmonic transposition or modulation from E♭ to B via C♭ works in the same way. To begin with, you have no idea what it *is*, much less how to do it. Follow the procedure, try and fail, slow down, simplify a crucial intermediate step, try again, and in due course you'll integrate the skill. Integration means passing from "It's impossible" to "It's easy," or more pertinently, "I'll never be able to do it" to "Sure, I can do it." More pertinently still, integration means passing from "I hate it" to "I love it."

Interaction of Color: The Albers Game

In his book *Interaction of Color*, originally published in 1963, Josef Albers studied and displayed a number of color juxtapositions, showing how our perception of a given color changes according to context. Red looks a certain way. Put it next to yellow, and your eyes feel that the red has changed. Put it next to purple, and the same red seemingly becomes yet another color.

You play something in C major, and you follow it by something else in E♭ major. Retroactively, you tweak your perception of C major; it feels to you as if C major "wasn't what you thought it was." E♭ has shined a special light on the preceding C major, delighting and surprising you.

The phenomenon also applies to forward movement. You play something in C, and you follow it with E♭: you feel something. You play the same thing in C, and you follow it with A♭: you feel something completely different.

You've practiced your Albers snippets, and you've learned how to transpose any snippet up by a minor third or down by a major third. Now you can start mixing and matching. Play one or two variations in a key of your choosing; move by a third up or down; play another one or two or three variations; move by a third up or down. Tweak rhythms if you wish. Add cadential formulas at the end. These juxtapositions and transpositions give you an unlimited database of improvisational and compositional possibilities.

Here are five of my combinations.

1. I took the Mixolydian segment starting in C, and I transposed it by ascending minor thirds (or their enharmonic equivalent): E♭, F♯, A, and back to C: "Rising Light" (example 8.31).

2. I mixed and matched the basic pattern, the Mixolydian variation, the sharp neighbor, and the minor version: "Yale Key" (example 8.32). Josef Albers taught at Yale University from 1950 to 1958.
3. I tweaked the rhythms and created a waltz-like composition with phrases of five bars: "Waltz for Anni" (example 8.33). Albers's wife Anni was an accomplished artist and scholar, a master of textile design and printmaking.
4. Using the Mixolydian variation, I created a journey passing through all twelve points of the circle of fifths: "Zwölf" (example 8.34). You'll notice that I didn't add dynamics, articulations, or tempo changes. It's all up to you.
5. I crossed the hands and introduced a melodic novelty: "Crossed Albers" (example 8.35)

EXAMPLE 8.31 "Rising Light" ©Pedro de Alcantara

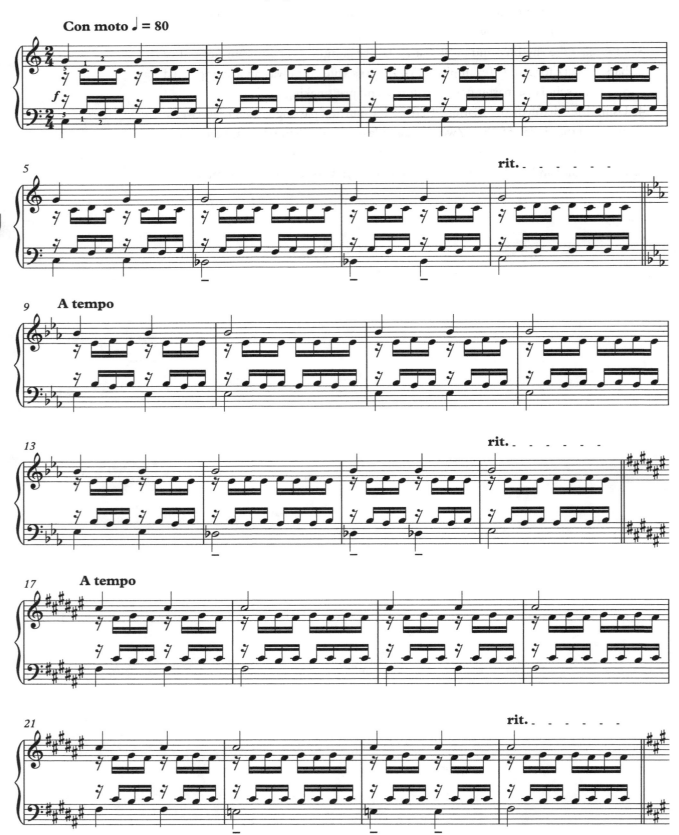

EXAMPLE 8.31 Continued

Creative Health for Pianists

EXAMPLE 8.32 "Yale Key" ©Pedro de Alcantara

EXAMPLE 8.32 Continued

Creative Health for Pianists

EXAMPLE 8.33 "Waltz for Anni" ©Pedro de Alcantara

EXAMPLE 8.33 Continued

EXAMPLE 8.34 "Zwölf" ©Pedro de Alcantara

EXAMPLE 8.34 Continued

Creative Health for Pianists

EXAMPLE 8.35 "Crossed Albers" ©Pedro de Alcantara

EXAMPLE 8.35 Continued

EXAMPLE 8.35 Continued

HORN CALL 9

Compositions
- Tuba Mirum (example 9.1)
- Valtorna (example 9.4)
- Double Valtorna (example 9.5)
- Klangbild I (example 9.6)
- Horn Call (example 9.7)
- Canyon (example 9.10)
- Trelliswork (example 9.17)
- Octane (example 9.18)
- Mahleriana (example 9.21)
- Mano Sinistra (example 9.22)
- Klangbild II (example 9.23)

Video Clips
- 40. Canyon
- 41. Mahleriana
- 42. Mano Sinistra

Our starting point consists of seven notes outlining an arpeggiated chord, which we assume is in B♭ major (example 9.1). Is it pretentious of me to call this very short snippet a composition? Yes, quite. But I consider it an archetype deserving of a thunderous title: "Tuba Mirum." I wrote down my preferred fingering, but it's only a suggestion. Put the gesture on a loop and repeat it many times.

EXAMPLE 9.1 "Tuba Mirum"

Creative Health for Pianists

What does *ff* mean? It's a trick question. What I really want to know is how do you think about it, how do you sense it, how do you play it? Use this arpeggio to find out who you are, in gesture and in sound.

You can bang at the piano with all your might, or you can discover how to get the piano to vibrate and resonate without your using much muscular effort. Indeed, muscular effort tends to prevent your sounds from being free and beautiful.

Test various gestures and postures. Slump low at the piano and play a loud arpeggio. Sit upright and relaxed, and play a loud arpeggio. Keep your wrist high and firm, lift your arm up above the keyboard, and throw everything down at the keys: your shoulder, your arm, your wrist. It's a "bang." Now keep your wrist low and relaxed, and hover your hand just above the keys. It takes skill, imagination, and courage to play *ff* in a state of containment and without banging.

Example 9.2 seems banal, but it hides some interesting possibilities. Play the arpeggio as before. Then play again and linger on every note, waiting until its sounds die down before striking the next note. Depending on the piano, the room acoustics, and your manner of playing, a single note may resonate for thirty seconds or longer. To linger, to wait, to listen without judging, to enjoy the moment without rushing onward: it's a meditation, and it may turn out to be difficult or enlightening or both.

After you do the meditation, play the arpeggio as originally written, with fermatas on two notes only. Your perception of the arpeggio, of yourself and of the world is now enhanced. You feel and hear things that you've never felt and heard before.

EXAMPLE 9.2 Fermatas

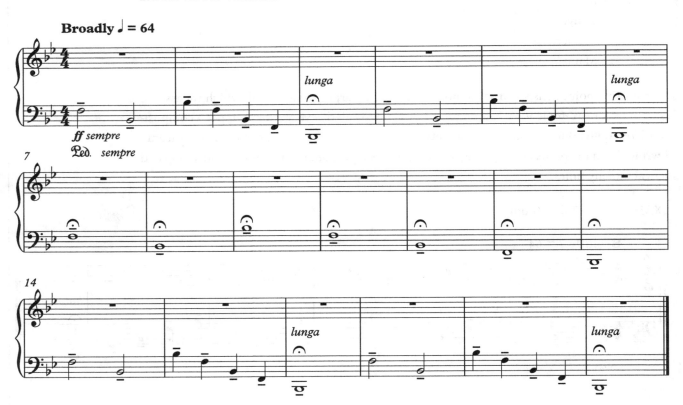

Remind yourself of note groupings. An iambic foot is preparation-STRESS: to BE | or NOT | to BE. A trochaic foot is STRESS-release: SAL-mon | HAD-dock | SEA bass. You can phrase the arpeggio of "Tuba Mirum" as either of them (example 9.3).

EXAMPLE 9.3 Iambic and trochaic groupings

Our current germinating seed or archetype explores, among other things, left-hand loudness and resonance; the interaction between gesture and sound; and the interaction of rhythm, note groupings, and sound. Being very simple, it lends itself to infinite variation in improvisations and compositions.

Let me show you two of my explorations. The first uses a musical tool we met in chapter 3: the superposition of two patterns of different lengths, one melodic and the other rhythmic (example 9.4). Rhythmic accents and downbeats will fall on different notes of the melodic pattern. I've titled this piece "Valtorna." You're not obliged to play the piece in constant *ff*, despite what the composer indicates in the score.

Creative Health for Pianists

EXAMPLE 9.4 "Valtorna" ©Pedro de Alcantara

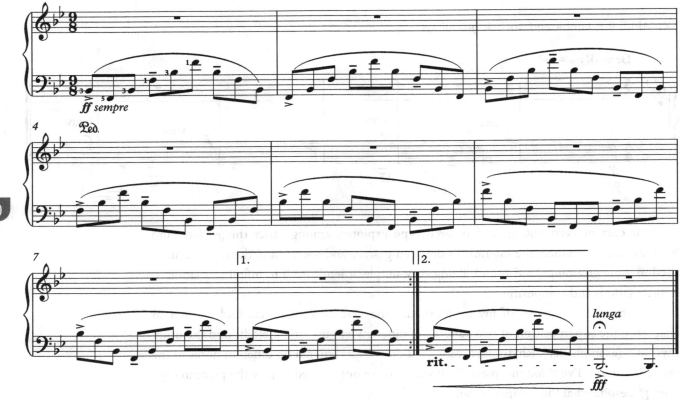

Like all patterns, it changes musically and technically according to how you group notes. Example 9.5 lays out two grouping possibilities, indicated by slurs, dynamics, and accents. One pattern is symmetrical, the other asymmetrical. It won't feel the same or sound the same. Let's call their juxtaposition "Double Valtorna."

EXAMPLE 9.5 "Double Valtorna" ©Pedro de Alcantara

My second improvisation-composition tweaks the starting pattern (example 9.6). You could learn and perform the set as a composition written in stone, unchangeable by fiat. Or you could take it apart, rearrange it, reorder its sections, repeat sections multiple times, insert your own variations, transpose some or all of it. Or you could summarize the archetype: "big beautiful sounds played by the left hand, regardless of how they're sequenced." Then you'd ignore my compositional efforts and create your own. I titled my set of variations "Klangbild I," using a fine German word with multiple connotations including *sonic image* and *acoustic pattern*.

EXAMPLE 9.6 "Klangbild I" ©Pedro de Alcantara

Horn Call

To our original left-hand pattern, we add a right-hand melody (example 9.7). I call this minuscule composition "Horn Call."

EXAMPLE 9.7 "Horn Call" ©Pedro de Alcantara

The horn call is an archetypal sound that sends you and your listeners on an imaginary trip to a forest and its hunting grounds. Versions of the horn call abound in classical music. Scarlatti, Mozart, Bruckner, and a hundred other composers have spun it into passages, sections, and whole works (figure 9.1).

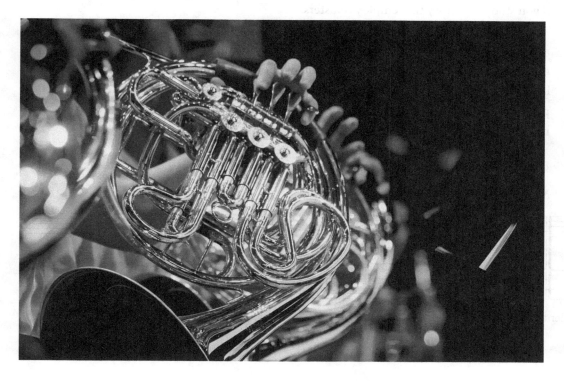

FIGURE 9.1 The Horn Call

Tempo, dynamics, timing, the balance of left and right hands: musically, your task is to go through every possible gradation and combination. Sitting relatively upright and relaxed, transferring weight from your back to your arm to your hand to your fingers to the keyboard, employing the least effort for the most effect: physically, your task is to enjoy practicing on an endless loop without boredom or frustration.

Example 9.8 introduces a new version of the horn call. Don't use the right pedal. Without sounding it, hold down a left-hand chord that includes the horn call pitches, an octave lower than the melody. On an acoustic piano, this creates shimmering sympathetic resonances, a magical and mysterious echo-like effect.

EXAMPLE 9.8 Sympathetic resonances

(hold down without sounding)

Instead of specific notes, now hold down a silent cluster (example 9.9). Place your left hand wide open across as many keys as possible, both black and white, encompassing the territory covered by the pitches in the preceding version. Press the keys down without sounding them, and hold this gesture as you play the horn call.

A cluster is a relatively modern innovation of piano technique. In piano scores, clusters are annotated in different styles. I chose one such style, but you'll come across other symbols if you study repertory that employs clusters.

You can use your hand *and* forearm together to hold down a larger number of notes. This magnifies the effect of sympathetic resonances. It'd complicate our scores if we tried to annotate each type of cluster with a different symbol: silent, not silent; white keys only, black keys only, mixed black and white; specific note range or not, hand or forearm . . . For practical purposes, we'll decide that our symbol means, "Hold down a silent cluster over many notes black and white, with left hand alone or with hand and forearm."

EXAMPLE 9.9 Cluster

(hold a silent cluster, including black and white keys)

Example 9.10 strings together various elements that we've practiced so far. I've titled it "Canyon." It contains a psychomotor challenge: timing the silent cluster and the actions of the right pedal. Place the cluster in measure 7 while still pressing the right pedal; release the pedal after you strike the first two notes of the horn call on the downbeat of measure 7; press down the right pedal again before placing the new silent cluster on measure 12; and so on. The score risks looking confusing to your eyes. Take it step by step, practice it a hundred times, and you'll get the hang of it. How deeply will you press the pedal? How gradually will you release it? What's happening to your toes and your ankle as you press and release the pedal?

Video Clip 40, "Canyon."

EXAMPLE 9.10 "Canyon" ©Pedro de Alcantara

Now we'll practice the skills of acoustic sensitivity. Play the horn call multiple times, without changing its tempo and dynamics (example 9.11). Instead, change right-hand articulations and what you do with the left hand and the pedal.

EXAMPLE 9.11 Acoustic sensitivity

(hold down without sounding)

(sustained silent cluster)

EXAMPLE 9.11 Continued

Creative Health for Pianists

Trelliswork

In life, it's possible to be oblivious to the marvelous; indifferent to it even when we see and hear it; or in awe of it, inspired and guided by it. Example 9.12 lays out a simple pattern for the left hand, in which we'll attempt to hear the marvelous. If we hear it, we can then decide whether we prefer to be indifferent or awed.

EXAMPLE 9.12 A rolling pattern

Will you make the two pitches even in color and articulation, or will you make the F louder and the B♭ softer, or vice versa? How much will you emphasize the downbeat? If you're sensitive to gradations, you can nuance this pattern endlessly.

To the left-hand pattern, we add the horn call (example 9.13). You can hold the right pedal down throughout, or hold it lightly, or vary it, or not use it. Don't let the composer's markings mislead you.

EXAMPLE 9.13 A rolling pattern with "Horn Call"

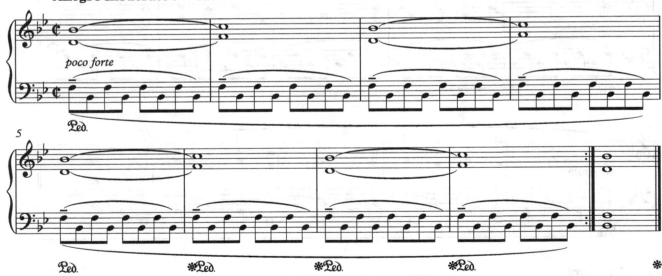

Our piece really is in four voices. Let's make it explicit (example 9.14).

EXAMPLE 9.14 A four-voice texture

Creative Health for Pianists

You'll remember from chapter 4 how each note or *fundamental* carries its own *harmonic series*. And you'll remember that the way you play a fundamental makes its harmonics more present or more hidden. Your touch, timing, articulation, inflection, perception, and intention contribute to give shape to the fundamental and to the harmonics that are inseparable from it.

Example 9.15 lays out the first eight harmonics for the B♭ and the F. You won't literally play them with your right hand; I'm only writing them on the upper staff for the sake of convenience. With practice, you can train yourself to distinguish, recognize, and name specific harmonics whenever you play a fundamental. To begin with, just play a repeated note with the sustaining pedal and listen.

EXAMPLE 9.15 Two fundamentals and their first eight harmonics

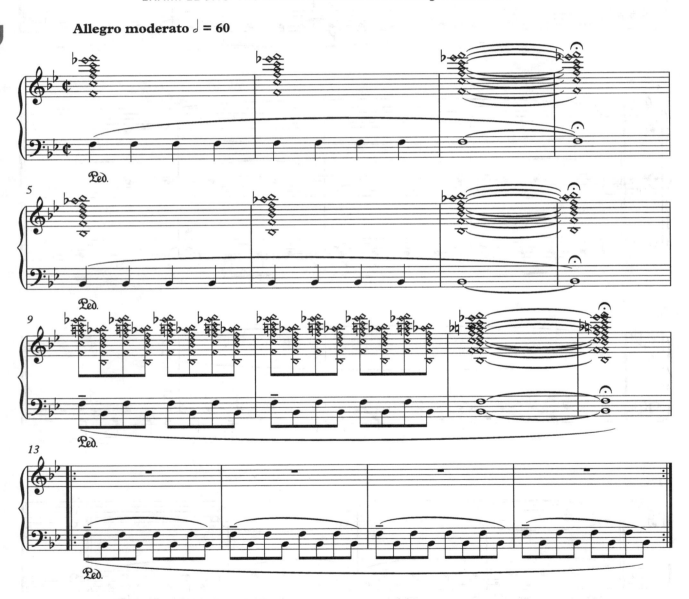

When you go back and forth quickly between the F and the B♭, you create an incredible festival of harmonics. You might not hear it, you might hear it and be indifferent or annoyed, or you might hear it and be entranced. The only certainty is that harmonics are *always* there, whenever you play one or more fundamentals. The music score only shows two pitches, an F and a B♭. But the sonic reality is infinitely richer.

Notice how the seventh harmonic of a B♭ is an A♭. (In reality, the actual harmonic is flatter, in sound, than the A♭ you'd play on an equal-tempered piano.) Musicians have always "heard" a fundamental's seventh harmonic. The quotes indicate that you can hear something sensorially and intuitively, without knowing intellectually that you're hearing it. The seventh harmonic "makes you want to play a B♭ major scale with a flat seventh." The intuition creates a musical structure prized in many types of music, including the blues and folk music all over the world. This is the *Mixolydian mode* (example 9.16). I like using it in my improvisations and compositions, as it's beautiful, caressing, and ambiguous.

Creative Health for Pianists

EXAMPLE 9.16 The Mixolydian mode

The first eight harmonics, numbered

Octave transpositions of harmonics 5 (D), 3 (F), and 7 (Ab)

The Mixolydian mode

A basic version of the 12-bar blues

We can now play the horn call above the marvelous rolling fifths (example 9.17). I like playing it relatively fast, but it's equally beautiful at a slower tempo. You might suspect that the composition isn't in B♭ major but in the Mixolydian mode. I've titled it "Trelliswork."

EXAMPLE 9.17 "Trelliswork" ©Pedro de Alcantara

Octane

Exercises, compositions, and improvisations can be separate entities, each with its personality; or they can be so close in character as to be indistinguishable. If you perform any exercise with care and commitment, the exercise "behaves" like a composition. If you play any composition with insight and freedom, the composition "behaves" like an improvisation. And if you practice skillfully in pleasure and joy, your practice "behaves" like a performance.

"Octane" lays out twelve segments of eight bars each, with a left-hand two-note drone and varied right-hand notes, patterns, and melodies including the horn call (example 9.18). Does it amount to a composition, or does it amount to a bunch of repetitive exercises of little musical merit? You decide. Is it boring, or is it beautiful? Should you use less pedal or more pedal? Should you put each segment on a loop with multiple repeats, and spend forty-five minutes lost to the composition's repetitive simplicity? Should you reorder the segments? Should you compose and improvise other melodies to be played against the unchanging drone? Should you change the drone? You decide. I call the composition "Octane." The meter seems tricky, but, look: the left hand won't ever change. The first segment, of left hand alone, allows you to practice the meter without worrying about the melodies.

EXAMPLE 9.18 "Octane" ©Pedro de Alcantara

Creative Health for Pianists

EXAMPLE 9.18 Continued

EXAMPLE 9.18 Continued

Creative Health for Pianists

EXAMPLE 9.18 Continued

Mahleriana and Mano Sinistra

Let's play a low drone in three voices, one of them syncopated (example 9.19). Johannes Brahms was known to enjoy this sort of effect, but since I'll soon paraphrase a snippet from Gustav Mahler's First Symphony, I'm naming our exercise-composition after Mahler.

EXAMPLE 9.19 Drone and syncopation

Although simple, the three-voice drone is rich in interpretive possibilities. In our imagination, we'll orchestrate it for viola, cello, and double bass, or three trombones, or any other plausible instrumental combination (example 9.20). In our practice, we'll master the inflections and dynamics of each independent voice. Since the left hand plays all voices, this is quite an interesting challenge.

EXAMPLE 9.20 Three-layered drone

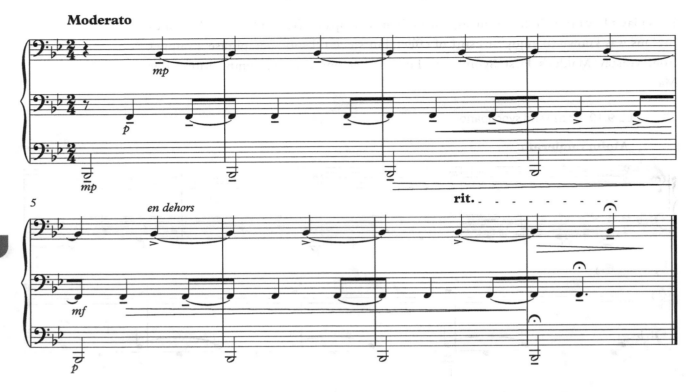

Above the drone we add melodies inspired by the horn call, and we'll title the result "Mahleriana" (example 9.21). This composition is modular, like many others in *Creative Health for Pianists*. The modules are numbered and separated by double bars. This makes it easier for you to make decisions as a co-composer: subtract a module, repeat a module, add your own. Do you find the low sounds murky and muddy? Play the whole thing an octave higher. You'll recognize "Frère Jacques" played in a minor key, as famously employed by Mahler in his First Symphony, which was premiered in 1889. I decided against writing in pedal markings or many dynamic indications. Interpretation and coloring are going to be up to you.

▶ Video Clip 41, "Mahleriana."

EXAMPLE 9.21 "Mahleriana" ©Pedro de Alcantara

EXAMPLE 9.21 Continued

EXAMPLE 9.21 Continued

"Mano Sinistra" is Italian for *left and* (example 9.22). We take a few ideas from "Mahleriana" and lay them out for the left hand alone.

Video Clip 42, "Mano Sinistra."

EXAMPLE 9.22 "Mano Sinistra" ©Pedro de Alcantara

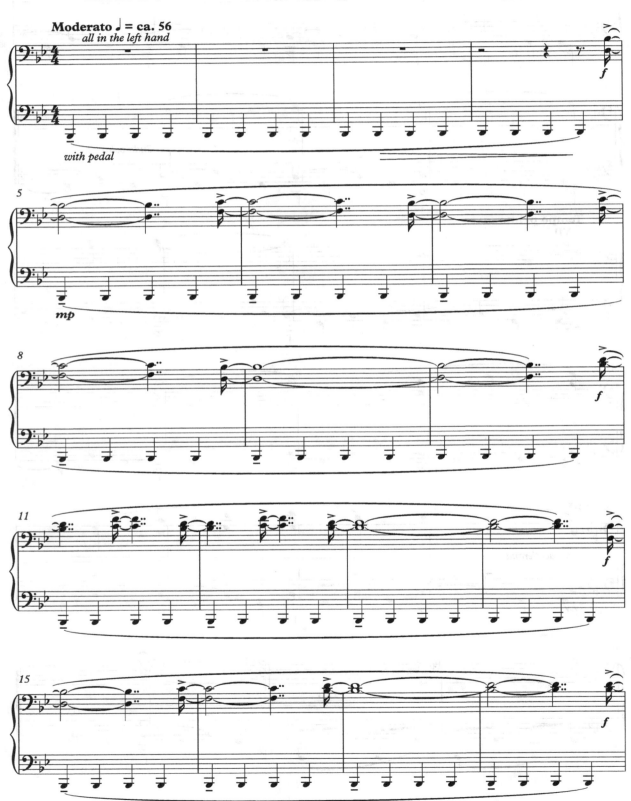

EXAMPLE 9.22 Continued

Klangbild II

Earlier on I introduced "Klangbild I" as a left-hand exploration of big sound. Let's add the right-hand horn call to it, and call it "Klangbild II" (example 9.23). This is another modular composition inviting you to tweak and rearrange it. Do you have access to a nice acoustic piano with a soft pedal (*una corda*)? It'd be wonderful to play some or all of the soft sections *una corda*.

EXAMPLE 9.23 "Klangbild II" ©Pedro de Alcantara

Creative Health for Pianists

EXAMPLE 9.23 Continued

The Horn Call Suite

In this chapter I've shared eleven compositions of varying lengths, from six bars to four pages. Here's a reminder of the compositions, in the order in which I introduced them.

1. Tuba Mirum
2. Valtorna
3. Double Valtorna
4. Klangbild I
5. Horn Call
6. Canyon
7. Trelliswork
8. Octane
9. Mahleriana
10. Mano Sinistra
11. Klangbild II

Let's suppose you enjoy studying, learning, mastering, and perhaps memorizing these compositions. Why not perform them in some sort of sequence? We'll call it the "Horn Call Suite." Include all compositions in your suite, or exclude one or more. Perform the sequence as laid out, or re-arrange its order. Many of the compositions are modular, and they lend themselves to shrinking and expanding according to your taste. When you add repeats and improvisations, the number of possible combinations and permutation of the "Horn Call Suite" is incalculable. You can go on a concert tour of 150 cities worldwide and never play the same suite twice.

By the way, it's not obligatory to play it by memory. It's often said that Franz Liszt (1811–1886), the composer and pianist, pioneered the skills of performing memorized compositions. If this is true, it means that Bach, Beethoven, Mozart, and Schubert probably used scores in their own performances. And many modern performers have used scores in their solo performances too.

The "Horn Call Suite" speaks of resonance, consonance and dissonance, vibrations and oscillations, forests, mountains, canyons, mysterious reverberations, heroic deeds, loneliness, and much else besides. Ovid tells the tale of Echo in his *Metamorphoses*. She was a beautiful, talkative nymph whose magnificent voice and song were much admired, including by Venus. Echo tricked Juno into believing that Juno's husband Jupiter was out of town, when in fact he was cavorting with other nymphs. Echo's trick allowed the nymphs to run away to safety. Juno decided to punish Echo, and caused her to lose the ability to speak as herself; instead, she'd only be able to repeat the last few words of a sentence spoken by someone else. Echo fell in love with Narcissus, but you know how their courtship went. "Who's there?" Narcissus said after detecting a presence in the woods. "Who's there?" Echo replied. "We must come together," he said. "We must come together," she said. Narcissus was in love with himself, of course, and eventually drowned while looking at his own reflection. Echo lost her beauty and turned into stone. All that is left of her is the sound of her voice.

Some compositions in the "Horn Call Suite" are sweet and tender ("Mahleriana"), others are raucous ("Klangbild I"), some are mysterious ("Canyon"), others are celebratory ("Octane"). Depending on how you organize your selections, you'll tell a story of fear or a story of hope. You don't have to think of Echo as you build your version of the "Horn Call Suite." It's only a prompt to help you explore the narrative potential of your music-making.

Do you need a suggested "Horn Call Suite" to get you going? Here it is.

The Horn Call Suite

I. Canyon
II. Double Valtorna
III. Klangbild II
IV. Mano Sinistra

MUDRA 10

Compositions
- Aristerá (example 10.12)
- Arvan (example 10.14)
- Gemini (example 10.17)
- Tallinn (example 10.18)
- Shapeshifter (example 10.20)
- Kaliště (example 10.22)
- Cats & Dogs (example 10.23)
- Vázlat (example 10.25)
- Nancarrow's Day Off (example 10.26)
- Brasilia (example 10.27)
- Transfiguration (example 10.28)
- Venus Rising (example 10.29)

Video clips
- 43. Mudra
- 44. Shapeshifter
- 45. Kaliště
- 46. Cats & Dogs
- 47. Venus Rising

Our starting point or archetype is an innocent-looking five-note chord, which I'm calling "Mudra" (example 10.1). We could analyze it as a dominant-ninth chord in the key of E♭, although "Mudra" has other identities as well.

EXAMPLE 10.1 Mudra

It may surprise you to see such a simple chord this late in the book, but I'm using the chord as a portal to enter a territory charged with mysteries.

Our existence contains a material dimension and a symbolic dimension. Flesh and bones, digestion and locomotion, jobs and taxes might be called material elements. Our occupation of time and space, our questions about fate and destiny, our thirst for love and beauty represent the symbolic dimension. The dimensions aren't separate. One pulls on the other, one feeds the other.

Playing the piano has its obvious material dimensions, starting with the piano itself, which is made of its own flesh and bones. Postures and positions, notes, fingerings, mechanisms, springs, weights and counterweights are some of the material aspects of the piano and the pianist. Just as obviously, piano playing has its symbolic dimensions. To set vibrations and oscillations in motion, to give life to a composition from three hundred years ago, to drink from the creative source . . . it's an unfathomable mystery (figure 10.1).

FIGURE 10.1 Mudra

There are different ways of defining the word *mudra*. I'll speak informally. Imagine a dancer in a temple somewhere in Southeast Asia—let's say Cambodia, perhaps not the actual country but the Cambodia of our imagination. The dancer moves slowly amidst the stone ruins overtaken by the jungle. She lifts her arms and hands, rotates them, brings her hands together and then apart again, her fingers gathering in exquisite positions. Her gestures are deeply felt, in sync with the land and the temple. Each of her hand positions says something beautiful and meaningful. The hands and the dance, the temple and the jungle form a coherent, organic, and blissful whole.

We'll call each of her meaningful and beautiful hand positions a *mudra*. The word comes from Sanskrit, where it originally meant *seal*, *mark*, or *gesture*. Mudras are systematized in different traditions, including Hinduism, Jainism, and Buddhism, as well as yoga and Indian dance. In mudras, the material and the symbolic dimensions are one and the same. Always speaking informally, I'll say that in some schools of thought there exists a specific number of mudras, each with a single, specific meaning; in other schools, it's considered that the number of mudras is uncounted and uncountable, because every hand position and every movement of every finger is considered sacred.

The notion that gestures and hand positions have spiritual power is shared across cultures. In everyday life, we use our hands in a thousand different ways, to handle objects and to touch people, to sense, to understand, to communicate. In truth, we don't need to go to our imaginary Cambodia to sense how powerful our hands are, and how meaningful their behavior is. A simple handshake carries a considerable emotional charge and illustrates the principle. I use the word *mudra* as a convenient abbreviation for a multilayered process (figure 10.2).

FIGURE 10.2 The master and the learner

Stability, Elasticity, and the Sonic Context

Every chord playable at the piano is a useful starting point for the exploration of the material and symbolic dimensions of piano playing. Our specific chord, however, has many merits. It engages all fingers, using a combination of black and white keys. It demands thought and attention, but isn't difficult to play. It allows the hand to organize itself as a stable entity. In sum, it creates a *whole-hand experience*. In addition, its sounds are beautiful and somewhat ambiguous.

Using the right pedal, play the chord repeatedly at a moderate speed (example 10.2). The whole-hand feeling of a stable structure meets the elastic surface of the keyboard, which becomes like a trampoline. The left hand provides some depth to the sonic context. Stability, elasticity, and soundscape become intertwined.

EXAMPLE 10.2 Whole-hand and trampoline

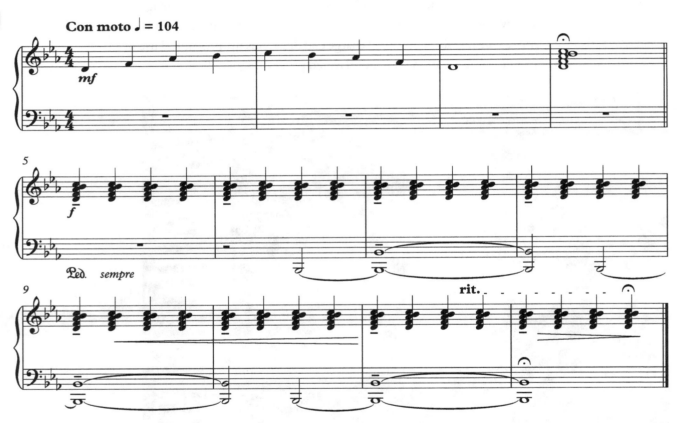

Music notation offers multiple ways of displaying this chord. You can put the flats in the key signature or in the score itself. There are legitimate reasons to choose one or the other, depending on context. Example 10.3 illustrates three possibilities.

EXAMPLE 10.3 Three ways of annotating a pattern

The chord may be heard as a dominant chord in E♭ major, with added seventh and ninth. But it could also be played and sensed in a modal context, in which the notion of dominant chords doesn't apply. Example 10.4 shows these two identities.

EXAMPLE 10.4 Two identities

The chord's apparent fixity as a hand position is relative. Example 10.5 moves us in and out of the hand position that we originally called a mudra. This marks the start of our exploration of the mudra's changeability.

Video Clip 43, "Mudra."

Creative Health for Pianists

EXAMPLE 10.5 Changeability

A whole-hand experience doesn't mean that individual fingers don't have their own intelligence. Example 10.6 lays out a sequence to enhance the initiative of each finger in turn.

EXAMPLE 10.6 Individual initiative

The work principle that we're developing is straightforward: take a chord and become extremely attentive to it. Example 10.7 makes things a little more complicated by juxtaposing rhythmic patterns to the repeated chord.

Creative Health for Pianists

EXAMPLE 10.7 Rhythmic patterns for practice

In our chord, each finger is assigned a specific note. But every finger remains available to play other notes within its reach (example 10.8).

EXAMPLE 10.8 Finger availability

Practice these exercises with caution, without rushing and without forcing. You're not doing finger calisthenics. Rather, you're caressing the keyboard expressively.

The Left-hand Mudra

The left-hand version of our starting mudra follows the original as regards distances between fingers, but the intervals are inversed (example 10.9).

EXAMPLE 10.9 Left-hand mudra

With the left hand, practice the exercises we've explored with the right hand: the feeling of the hand bouncing on the trampoline-keyboard, the voicings and rhythms. Here I limit myself to laying out the exercise in which fingers seek their freedom of movement within the position (example 10.10). Caresses, not calisthenics!

EXAMPLE 10.10 Left-hand finger availability

Creative Health for Pianists

Example 10.11 presents a new mudra—that is, a new archetypal territory to be explored. Example 10.12 develops it as a composition, which I've titled "Aristerá" (Greek for *left*). The composition is modular, organized in phrases of eight bars. Isolate a phrase and practice it as a self-contained entity. If a phrase seems too difficult, eliminate it from the composition or postpone working on it until you feel ready. Pedaling would allow you to relax your hand from bar to bar.

EXAMPLE 10.11 An archetype

EXAMPLE 10.12 "Aristerá" ©Pedro de Alcantara

Creative Health for Pianists

EXAMPLE 10.12 Continued

Practice the same piece, but inverting the rhythmic relationship between melody and drone. Example 10.13 is a snippet of the inverted relationship.

EXAMPLE 10.13 Inverted relationship

Beyond the Entry Point

Imagine a huge maze with thousands of paths leading to a central destination, each path with its own entry point. It's impossible to determine what's the best entry point. Instead, you need to *agree to enter*, via any entry point. For the exploration of mudra, I chose as my entry point the right-hand chord that looks like a dominant-ninth chord in E♭ major. If you're literal-minded, you risk thinking that this chord is "the mudra." No; this chord is one among many possible entry points into the mudra maze.

But now that we've entered the maze through this one entry point, we're going to dwell in the company of the chord—this mudra of comfort, pleasure, and musical ambiguity. We'll use compositions from earlier chapters to deepen our sense of what this mudra feels like, what we can do with it musically, and how it becomes transformed by sonic and rhythmic contexts.

We'll take the seesaw pattern in $\frac{12}{8}$ that we used in chapter 3, and we'll marry it to our mudra (example 10.14). I call this composition "Arvan," which is Sanskrit for *horse*. The first two bars, marked *a piacere*, are optional. Consider them an invitation for you to improvise a preluding arpeggio before launching the piece.

EXAMPLE 10.14 "Arvan" ©Pedro de Alcantara

Apply the same process to the left-hand version of the mudra. Example 10.15 shows a little snippet of it.

EXAMPLE 10.15 Left-hand "Arvan"

You may remember another composition from chapter 3, where we pressed down keys with the left hand without sounding their notes. (Look up example 3.13 to refresh your memory.) We'll adapt this compositional principle to our current exploration. Example 10.16 sets out the beginning of the new composition. Feel free to continue it, to improvise its development, and to title it as you wish.

EXAMPLE 10.16 Mudra and sympathetic resonances

The original left-hand mudra clashes sonically with the original right-hand mudra if we play both at the same time. Instead, we'll find a left-hand pattern that fits nicely with the right hand. In the second half of the piece, we'll introduce a clever little difficulty. It's part of our working method: Is something too easy? Spice it up. Is something too complicated? Rewrite it. Would you like to seem pretentious to your peers? Give your modest compositions mystical-sounding names. This one I call "Gemini" (example 10.17).

Creative Health for Pianists

EXAMPLE 10.17 "Gemini" ©Pedro de Alcantara

Also in chapter 3, I presented a variation of the seesaw pattern in which you keep your thumbs down after they sound their notes. It's sonically interesting, and it stabilizes the hand. Back then, I called the resulting composition "In Estonia." Let's name this one after Estonia's capital, "Tallinn" (example 10.18). You might enjoy pedaling it.

EXAMPLE 10.18 "Tallinn" ©Pedro de Alcantara

Example 10.19 shows a snippet of the same composition, adapted to the left hand. Finish it to your liking.

EXAMPLE 10.19 Left-hand "Tallinn"

Transformation

As a hand position, the mudra is easily transformed. All you need to do is to change one or more notes of the chord associated with it. Example 10.20 shows our original mudra undergoing a few gradual changes, creating a sequence of related mudras. Put on a loop, transpose it up or down an octave or two, tweak the dynamics, the pedaling, and the voicing. Then you have a composition: "Shapeshifter."

▶ Video Clip 44, "Shapeshifter."

EXAMPLE 10.20 "Shapeshifter" ©Pedro de Alcantara

Example 10.21 shows a sort of warm-up exercise preparing the hand to become adaptable.

EXAMPLE 10.21 Preparation

In chapter 9, we juxtaposed the horn call and a left-hand three-voice drone. The result was "Mahleriana." Here we'll employ a similar starting point. The composition is modular, inviting you to repeat phrases, add or subtract sections, transpose a phrase an octave up or down, and so on. It's called "Kaliště," the town of Gustav Mahler's birth in Bohemia (example 10.22). Do you like giving yourself ambitious tasks? Transpose this piece along the circle of fifths, preferably on the counterclockwise journey. Play it key by key in sequence: two flats, three flats, four flats, and so on. It's like a musical coloring book, over which you can display your control of dynamics, inflections, pedaling, embellishments, and so on.

Video Clip 45, "Kaliště."

Creative Health for Pianists

EXAMPLE 10.22 "Kaliště" ©Pedro de Alcantara

Three against Two

Over the decades, I've met a number of musicians who have a phobia of three-against-two. I like example 10.23 well enough to deem it a composition and title it "Cats & Dogs." You might want to consider it a barebones trigger for you to improvise or compose something much more elaborate.

EXAMPLE 10.23 "Cats & Dogs" ©Pedro de Alcantara

A phobia is a combination of fear and hatred. The feeling of three-against-two can be elusive. The hands and fingers don't obey the brain. The brain itself doesn't obey the brain! Or perhaps the brain is quite obedient: it responds to the fear in you and gives fearful commands to the hands and fingers. Let's invent a new theory, with no backing from neuroscience. There's a part of your brain that deals in "two," and a different part of your brain that deals in "three." Three-against-two is a fight between two disparate mental functions. When you find the feeling of it, you integrate these normally antagonistic functions. Dopamine starts flowing from the brain outward, and you start loving yourself and the world because you've become free from fear and hatred. To simplify a complex issue, we'll state that all learning is healing, and learning to play three-against-two heals you from a nagging phobia.

Start playing "Cats & Dogs." The "three" is doable. The "two" is doable. When three starts going against the two, you risk the frustration of failure, which (as we know) makes people insane. Get a friend or colleague to play it for you, or to try to play it for you. Let's suppose your friend suffers a phobic attack of frustration and failure. You'll see amazing sights and hear amazing sounds! A crescendo of frustration and an accelerando of failure! Scrunched neck! Obsessive banging! Bad words!

Creative Health for Pianists

You don't want to be like that, do you?

Decide that you'll work steadily, sometimes with a metronome, sometimes without; sometimes by feel, sometimes by counting. If you notice that you're getting frustrated, make a decision: Continue or pause? Fall into the temptation of frustration, or find a little distance from the trigger and the habit? "Cats & Dogs" looks like a nothing bit of nothing, but it's both the trigger and the possibility of overcoming the trigger. Its construction gives you the space you need in which to make these healing decisions.

One of the clues to solving the three-against-two conundrum is linguistic. What are they saying, the cat and the dog? What would happen if they talked at the same time? Their rhythms would juxtapose to create an interesting pattern. Example 10.24 shows you the linguistic pattern and how you might learn to speak three-against-two.

EXAMPLE 10.24 The linguistics of three-against-two

After you get the hang of it, superpose "Cats & Dogs" and our mudra (example 10.25). I title this composition "Vázlat," which is Hungarian for *sketch*. Put it on a loop, performing it with the metronome. Play it as written, then try transposing the right hand one octave down. In video clip 46 I show "Cats & Dogs" with a variety of articulations, accents, and timings, followed by a version of "Vázlat."

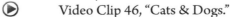   Video Clip 46, "Cats & Dogs."

EXAMPLE 10.25 "Vázlat" ©Pedro de Alcantara

In Chapter 9 we studied "Valtorna," built on the superposition of two patterns of different lengths, one melodic and the other rhythmic. Here we'll create a similar superposition (example 10.26). I'm calling the result "Nancarrow's Day Off." Conlon Nancarrow (1912–1997) was known for composing fantastically complicated pieces for player piano.

What can you do with "Nancarrow's Day Off"? My version of it employs three right-hand chords. It'd be easy to keep going and to employ other chords without altering the left hand in any way. And it'd be fun (though not necessarily easy) to change the left-hand chord at some point.

EXAMPLE 10.26 "Nancarrow's Day Off" ©Pedro de Alcantara

Creative Health for Pianists

EXAMPLE 10.26 Continued

Transfiguration

Let's be amateur metaphysicians for a moment. The deity wants to express a certain emotion, crystalized in a set of musical intervals gathered in a chord or an arpeggio. To manifest these intervals at the piano, the deity designs a hand shape, with distances among the fingers, stretches, arches, angles. The deity then chooses you as her expressive herald, and compels you to sit at the piano and produce the intervals that communicate her emotions. You think that you create emotions by shaping your hands and playing intervals and fingerings. But in fact it's the intervals that shape your hands, and they do so to express their own emotions.

Let's let the deity make us play a song with the left hand, based on that most marvelous of mudras: the first five notes of the E-major scale. I call it "Brasilia" (example 10.27). My left hand is big and stretchy, and I like sustaining the downbeat E throughout the bar, regardless of the intervals of the arpeggio that follows the downbeat. But there are so many ways of articulating and inflecting this short piece, with or without the right pedal, that you really don't have to sustain the E and hurt yourself in the process.

Creative Health for Pianists

EXAMPLE 10.27 "Brasilia" ©Pedro de Alcantara

We'll end the chapter and the book with a simple composition for the right hand alone. There are two versions of it: chord and arpeggio. The arpeggio version is easier to sight-read, but for my own reasons I want it to be the book's last page. I've titled the chord version "Transfiguration" (example 10.28) and the arpeggio version "Venus Rising" (example 10.29).

EXAMPLE 10.28 "Transfiguration" ©Pedro de Alcantara

Creative Health for Pianists

EXAMPLE 10.29 "Venus Rising" ©Pedro de Alcantara

Video Clip 47, "Venus Rising."

CONCLUSION

The piano is a shapeshifter. The instrument played by Vladimir Horowitz doesn't seem to be same instrument played by Thelonious Monk. Different sounds, different vibes, different emotions.

I think the piano changes to accommodate your personality and aesthetics. Be yourself, and the piano will be a natural and organic extension of who you are.

There exist mystically minded pianist-composers, such as Alexander Scriabin. There exist improvisers who specialize in playing fast notes with a delicate and witty touch, like the amazing Art Tatum. There exist intellectuals, jokesters, entertainers, extraverts, introverts, all sorts of pianists playing all sorts of pianos. Liberace, Victor Borge, Marta Argerich, Guiomar Novaes, Chick Corea, Yuja Wang, Ahmad Jamal, Hermeto Pascoal: you really can't mistake one for the other. Each is wonderful in a unique way.

Behind each pianist there's a story. Imagine a pianist who's a pure product of the Soviet system, and whose career serves the state ideology. Now imagine another Soviet pianist whose career is a heroic fight against the state ideology. These are two different stories, resulting in different pianists with different careers. Glenn Gould is inseparable from Glenn Gould's story. And Artur Rubinstein's story is inevitably different from Gould's. If you don't think there's a story behind Liberace, you don't know Liberace.

Thousands of years ago, Plato composed a political text for which he needed a subtle, illustrative argument. Therefore, he invented Atlantis—a civilization like no other, which allowed him to speak critically about his own culture through a process of comparison: Atlantis was perfect; Athens wasn't Atlantis; Athens wasn't perfect. Plato's invention took on a life of its own, and Atlantis became many things to many people. It became real, although as with everything real it exists in multiple versions. In one version, the island of Atlantis was an extremely advanced civilization, the home of incredible technologies and of accomplishments both individual and collective. Atlantis was located somewhere in the Atlantic Ocean, maybe near the island of Madeira, maybe near the Bermuda triangle. Unless it was located in the Mediterranean, or in the North Pole, or—well, somewhere. A catastrophic event destroyed Atlantis, probably an earthquake or seaquake. This happened 12,000 years ago, or maybe a few hundred years before Plato's lifetime, unless it happened at a difficult-to-determine point in history. And the survivors from the catastrophe scattered to the four corners of the

Conclusion

Earth, bringing with them remnants of their advanced culture and helping the Mayas and the Egyptians build their pyramids, a definitive demonstration of Atlantean prowess.

Plato was also known for his belief on the existence of archetypes, sometimes also called *universals* or *ideal forms*. It'd take us too long to define these terms and give them context. Instead, we'll simplify things and call an archetype a sort of force or energy that exists eternally and in a perfect state. The archetype manifests itself in an object, a person, an event, a story, and so on. To give a banal example, the archetype of red or redness manifests itself in a red rose, a red sunset, a red shirt, a red face, anything and everything that is red.

You know where I'm going with this, don't you? *Creative Health for Pianists* is based on a couple of dozen musical snippets which I've allowed myself to call archetypes (although technically I should have called each of them "an expression of an archetype," since the archetype itself exists on an immaterial, ideal plane). Each of my little archetypal expressions highlights a musical concept: consonance and dissonance, resonance and sympathetic vibrations, tendency notes, the harmonic series, the intertwining of intervals and finger movement, and so on. Being the manifestation of ideal forms, these archetypes lead you to become deeply sensitive to their underlying musical phenomena. Alertness, enjoyment, creativity, and pleasure combine to create a certain type of pianist—the type of musician who likes playing simple and beautiful things, and who learns to play them well and reliably. Not that you should limit yourself to playing simple things; this is only the starting point. Go anywhere you want!

Creative Health for Pianists comes from Atlantis, that beautiful imaginary island where medicine and music are one and the same, where a single note contains all notes, where music is discovery, connection, vibration, and healing. The great thing about Atlantis is that an individual can posit crazy and strange claims without being made to feel embarrassed about it. After all, the Atlantis music conservatory is called The House of Unconditional Love.

That's the story, anyway.

FIGURE C.1 Propagation

Video Clip 48, "Unconditional Love."

APPENDIX: PRACTICING THE CIRCLE OF FIFTHS

This appendix is a database that gathers a handful of tonal journeys mentioned in chapter 5.

It takes practice to internalize key signatures, which is necessary in mastering the circle of fifths and, more generally, the whole world of tonalities, relationships, and accidentals. A useful intermediate step is to read scales and chord progressions in which every accidental is written out right next to the affected note. This database has some sequences with key signatures, and some without.

What I show you in print is by no means what you're obliged to play. The appendix is a collection of reminders or aides-mémoire. You can and, in my opinion, you *must* be inventive and adaptable as regards your reaction to information. Suppose I throw something hairy at you, like a densely displayed scale and chord progression in G♯ minor, without the key signature (example A.1).

EXAMPLE A.1 A threat

It looks "wild" and "hostile" to you. Then you have to "tame it" and "befriend it." Streamline it, stretch it, slow it down, and play it not as a difficult technical exercise but as a lyrical little composition (example A.2).

Appendix

EXAMPLE A.2 A change in perspective

I'll take a diatonic circle of fifths and make something up (example A.3). My practice starts with the diatonic circle of fifths in D minor, served straight up. I tweak the rhythm. I add sevenths to every second bar. I bring an improvisatory edge to the left hand. Finally, I give it a clever title: "Thelonious, Age Seven." I might apply a similar approach to every bit of information in the appendix.

EXAMPLE A.3 "Thelonious, Age Seven"

Appendix

The contents of the database are displayed in the order they're mentioned in chapter 5.

1. The *circle of fifths progression*, also known as the *diatonic circle of fifths*, in all major and minor keys. Two versions: first without key signature changes (example A.4), then with changes (example A.5).
2. The famous diddle, without key signature changes (example A.6).
3. A one-octave scale followed by a brief chord progression, in all major and minor keys, without key signature changes (example A.7).
4. "Dialogue." Twelve keys, with key signature changes (example A.8).
5. "Heartbreak." Twelve keys, without signature changes (example A.9).

EXAMPLE A.4 The circle of fifths progression, without key signature changes

Appendix

EXAMPLE A.4 Continued

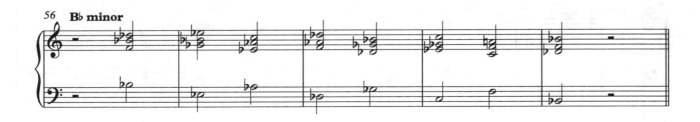

EXAMPLE A.4 Continued

Appendix

EXAMPLE A.4 Continued

EXAMPLE A.5 The circle of fifths progression, with key signature changes

Appendix

EXAMPLE A.5 Continued

Appendix

EXAMPLE A.5 Continued

Appendix

EXAMPLE A.5 Continued

Appendix

EXAMPLE A.6 The famous diddle, without key signature changes

Appendix

EXAMPLE A.7 A scale and a progression in all keys

EXAMPLE A.7 Continued

Appendix

EXAMPLE A.7 Continued

EXAMPLE A.7 Continued

Appendix

EXAMPLE A.8 "Dialogue" in twelve keys, with key signature changes

EXAMPLE A.9 "Heartbreak" in twelve keys, without key signature changes

Appendix

EXAMPLE A.9 Continued

Resources

To illustrate the all-welcoming reach of *Creative Health for Pianists* I invited friends, colleagues, and strangers to contribute performances of some of my compositions. To my delight and eternal gratitude, concert pianists, piano teachers, beginners, amateurs, the confident and the diffident took part. Their clips cover perhaps 70 or 80 percent of the book's basic materials, though of course not the infinite variations that the materials allow for. There are professionally recorded performances, smartphone home videos, baby grands, uprights, electronic keyboards, a harpsichord, an accordion, a guitar.

These clips are hosted on my website. Please visit www.pedrodealcantara.com/piano.

Below are the pieces from my friends and collaborators, identified by title and placement within the book. A second list groups the pieces by performer rather than by chapter.

Unless otherwise indicated, recordings use a piano or an electronic keyboard. Performers have sometimes added embellishments, tweaks, transpositions, and improvisations. This is a natural part of music making, and I explicitly encourage it in *Creative Health for Pianists*. On various occasions the performers offer two or more interpretations of the same piece, making changes to tempo, articulation, dynamics, and pedaling. This, too, is completely natural and to be encouraged. A few pieces have been recorded by more than one performer.

I hope you'll enjoy seeing and hearing what your fellow explorers have done with my modest creations.

The performances:

Chapter 1 "Dialogue"
- 1.12 Trivium: Alison Roper-Lowe
- 1.15 Promenade: Carla Marchesini
- 1.23 Seksy Sesky: Petra Lipinski
- 1.24 Tally Up: Jon Breaux, piano and guitar
- 1.26 Pentagram: Lara Erbès
- 1.31 Brief Eulogy: Carla Marchesini
- 1.32 Eulogy: Petra Lipinski
- 1.35 Driven: Carla Marchesini
- 1.36 Driven Forward: Helen Kashap
- 1.39 Charanga: Lorenzo Marasso
- 1.40 Jumping Frog: Lara Erbès
- 1.41 Juventud: Rosana Civile
- 1.42 Tranquil: Petra Lipinski
- 1.43 Farewell: Viki Roth

Chapter 2 "Heartbreak"
- 2.6 Cycle of Heartbreak: Carla Marchesini
- 2.12 Muster: Magdalena Portmann, accordion

Resources

    2.13 Little Chorale: Dellal McDonald
    2.14 Chorale: Dellal McDonald
    2.23 Afternoon Waltz: Carla Marchesini
    2.24 Carezza: Petra Lipinski
    2.29 Janus: Karolina Glab
    2.30 Cradle: Mona Al-Kazemi
    2.30 Cradle: Helen Kashap
    2.33 I Plead with Thee: Viki Roth
    2.34 Ascension: Helen Kashap
    2.36 Easy Easy: Jon Breaux
    2.36 Easy Easy: Carla Marchesini
    2.37 Not Too Easy: Lara Erbès
    2.37 Not Too Easy: Dellal McDonald
    2.37 Not Too Easy: Dellal McDonald, harpsichord

Chapter 3 "Seesaw"
    3.6 Together Apart: Bonnie Lubinsky
    3.12 Arabian Horse: Dellal McDonald
    3.12 Arabian Horse: Dellal McDonald, harpsichord
    3.13 Marrakesh: Lorenzo Marasso
    3.16 Im Nebel Gesehen: Karolina Glab
    3.17 Im Nebel Schwach Gesehen: Karolina Glab

Chapter 4 "Celeste"
    4.6 "Celeste" Theme and Variations: Lorenzo Marasso
    4.20 Grace: Karolina Glab
    4.22 Pacific Sunrise: Rosana Civile
    4.23 Celestial: In Memoriam ABM: Lorenzo Marasso

Chapter 5 "The Circle"
    5.7 Émile: Karolina Glab

Chapter 6 "Gesture"
    6.5 Sergei's Warm-up: Petra Lipinski
    6.6 Sergei: Rosana Civile
    6.6 Sergei: Karolina Glab
    6.11 Light and Shadow: Mona Al-Kazemi
    6.12 Respect: Jon Breaux
    6.15 Thimble: Petra Lipinski
    6.18 Remorse: Karolina Glab
    6.20 Mikro: Petra Lipinski
    6.21 Love Left: Karolina Glab
    6.22 Envelope: Rosana Civile
    6.23 Love Right: Jorge Baeza Stanicic

Chapter 7 "Advanced Seesaw"
- 7.8 Piper: Dellal McDonald
- 7.8 Piper: Alison Roper-Lowe
- 7.9 Cloverleaf Piper: Mona Al-Kazemi
- 7.11 The Twelve: Rosana Civile
- 7.11 The Twelve: Lorenzo Marasso
- 7.24 Odd Man Blues: Jorge Baeza Stanicic
- 7.26 Catch the Breeze: Helen Kashap
- 7.26 Catch the Breeze: Carla Marchesini
- 7.27 Breezy: Dellal McDonald
- 7.27 Breezy: Dellal McDonald, harpsichord

Chapter 8 "Sonic Play"
- 8.12 Skend: Rosana Civile
- 8.12 Skend: Petra Lipinski
- 8.13 Serpentipedi: Helen Kashap
- 8.14 Iocus: Dellal McDonald
- 8.14 Iocus: Dellal McDonald, harpsichord
- 8.16 Quest: Lara Erbès
- 8.18 Composure: Viki Roth
- 8.31 Rising Light: Jorge Baeza Stanicic
- 8.32 Yale Key: Dellal McDonald
- 8.32 Yale Key: Dellal McDonald, harpsichord
- 8.33 Waltz for Anni: Lorenzo Marasso
- 8.34 Zwölf: Jorge Baeza Stanicic
- 8.35 Crossed Albers: Lorenzo Marasso

Chapter 9 "Horn Call"
- 9.5 Double Valtorna: Renato Figueiredo
- 9.7 Horn Call: Renato Figueiredo
- 9.10 Canyon: Rosana Civile
- 9.17 Trelliswork: Mona Al-Kazemi
- 9.18 Octane: Rosana Civile
- 9.21 Mahleriana: Lorenzo Marasso
- 9.22 Mano Sinistra: Renato Figueiredo
- 9.23 Klangbild II: Renato Figueiredo
- 9.23 Klangbild II: Karolina Glab
- Horn Call Suite: Renato Figueiredo
    - I. Horn Call
    - II. Valtorna
    - III. Klangbild II
    - IV. Mano Sinistra

Resources

Chapter 10 "Mudra"
    10.12 Aristerá: Rosana Civile
    10.14 Arvan: Helen Kashap
    10.14 Arvan: Dellal McDonald
    10.14 Arvan: Dellal McDonald, harpsichord
    10.17 Gemini: Jorge Baeza Stanicic
    10.18 Tallinn: Rosana Civile
    10.18 Tallinn: Karolina Glab
    10.25 Vázlat: Rosana Civile
    10.26 Nancarrow's Day Off: Lorenzo Marasso
    10.28 Transfiguration: Viki Roth

Appendix
    A.3   Thelonious, Age Seven (Alison Roper-Lowe)

The performers:

  Mona Al-Kazemi, amateur pianist and teacher of the Alexander Technique
    2.30 Cradle
    6.11 Light and Shadow
    7.9   Cloverleaf Piper
    9.17 Trelliswork

  Jorge Baeza Stanicic, pianist and teacher
    6.23 Love Right
    7.24 Odd Man Blues
    8.31 Rising Light
    8.34 Zwölf
    10.17 Gemini

  Jon Breaux
    1.24 Tally Up (piano and guitar)
    2.36 Easy Easy
    6.12 Respect

  Rosana Civile, pianist and teacher
    1.41 Juventud
    4.22 Pacific Sunrise
    6.6   Sergei
    6.22 Envelop
    7.11 The Twelve
    8.12 Skend
    9.10 Canyon
    9.18 Octane
    10.12 Aristerá
    10.18 Tallinn
    10.25 Vázlat

Lara Erbès, concert pianist and teacher
- 1.26 Pentagram
- 1.40 Jumping Frog
- 2.37 Not Too Easy
- 8.16 Quest

Renato Figueiredo, pianist
- 9.4 Double Valtorna
- 9.7 Horn Call
- 9.22 Mano Sinistra
- 9.23 Klangbild II

"Horn Call Suite"
- I Horn Call
- II Double Valtorna
- III Klangbild II
- IV Mano Sinistra

Karolina Glab, pianist and teacher
- 2.29 Janus
- 3.16 In Nebel Gesehen
- 3.17 In Nebel Schwach Gesehen
- 4.20 Grace
- 5.7 Émile
- 6.6 Sergei
- 6.18 Remorse
- 6.21 Love Left
- 9.23 Klangbild II
- 10.18 Tallinn

Helen Kashap, concert pianist ant teacher
- 1.36 Driven Forward
- 2.30 Cradle
- 2.34 Ascension
- 7.26 Catch the Breeze
- 8.13 Serpentipedi
- 10.14 Arvan

Petra Lipinski, professional violinist
- 1.23 Seksy Sesky
- 1.32 Eulogy
- 1.42 Tranquil
- 2.24 Carezza
- 6.5 Sergei's Warm-up
- 6.15 Thimble
- 6.20 Mikro
- 8.12 Skend

Resources

Bonnie Lubinsky, professional flutist
- 3.6 Together Apart

Lorenzo Marasso, concert pianist, conductor, and radio host
- 1.39 Charanga
- 3.13 Marrakesh
- 4.6 "Celeste" Theme and Variations
- 4.23 In Memoriam ABM
- 7.11 The Twelve
- 8.23 Waltz for Anni
- 8.35 Crossed Albers
- 9.21 Mahleriana
- 10.26 Nancarrow's Day Off

Carla Marchesini, painter, poet, and pianist
- 1.15 Promenade
- 1.31 Brief Eulogy
- 1.35 Driven
- 2.6 Cycle of Heartbreak
- 2.23 Afternoon Waltz
- 2.36 Easy Easy
- 7.26 Catch the Breeze

Dellal McDonald, pianist and harpsichordist
- Piano:
  - 2.13 Little Chorale
  - 2.14 Chorale
  - 2.37 Not Too Easy
  - 3.12 Arabian Horse
  - 7.8 Piper
  - 7.27 Breezy
  - 8.14 Iocus
  - 8.32 Yale Key
  - 10.14 Arvan
- Harpsichord:
  - 2.37 Not Too Easy
  - 3.12 Arabian Horse
  - 7.27 Breezy
  - 8.14 Iocus
  - 8.32 Yale Key
  - 10.14 Arvan

Magdalena Portmann, creative explorer
- 2.12 Muster (accordion)

Alison Roper-Lowe, teacher of the Alexander Technique
- 1.12 Trivium
- 7.8 Piper
- A.3 Thelonious, Age Seven

Viki Roth, arts administrator and pianist
- 1.43 Farewell
- 2.33 I Plead with Thee
- 8.18 Composure
- 10.28 Transfiguration

Index

For the benefit of digital users, indexed terms that span two pages (e.g., 52–53) may, on occasion, appear on only one of those pages.

Figures are indicated by *f* following the page number

acoustics, 156, 305
"Albers" (musical archetype)
    ambiguity, 274*f*
    game, 284–96
    sequence, 278*f*
    sympathetic vibrations, 273*f*
    transposition, 275*f*
        enharmonic, 282–84
        by thirds, 279–81
    variations, 275–78
Albers, Anni, 285
Albers, Josef, 272, 284
    Interaction of Color, 284
archetype, 1, 6, 11, 29–42, 43–44, 85, 104, 138, 147, 170, 175, 191, 192, 196, 238, 255, 269, 272, 275, 297, 299, 303, 331, 342, 364
Atlantis, 363–64

Bartók, Béla, 204
    Mikrokosmos, 204
bilateral transfer, 215
blues, 311, 312*f*
Bolet, Jorge, 129
bounce, 36*f*, 94–95
building block, 22, 241, 255, 263

"Celeste" (musical archetype)
    gradations, 109
    harmonic series, 123–24
    note grouping, 107*f*
    sonic materials, 110*f*
    spinning sounds, 107–10
    variations, 111–16
    voicing, 126–28
circle of fifths
    accidentals, 162–65
    Chartres Cathedral, 154*f*
    chord progressions, 167*f*
    circle of fifths progression, 160–61
    conscientious practice, 166–69
    counterclockwise journey, 155–60
    enharmonic passage, 154–55
    layers of the keyboard, 154*f*
    manifold, 151*f*
    tendency tones, 162*f*
    tonal relationships, 153–54
    twelve (the number), 153–54
clashes and caresses, 10–11, 19, 20, 124, 130–39, 140
cluster, 118–19, 304
comfort, 1, 11*f*, 44, 99, 117, 153, 215, 345
compositions
    Afternoon Waltz, 63*f*
    The Albers Sequence, 278*f*
    Aloysia, 227*f*
    Aloysia's Accidental Travels, 236*f*
    Aloysia's Travels, 234*f*
    Amby, 193*f*
    Arabian Horse, 97*f*
    Archimedes, 161*f*
    Aristerá, 343*f*
    Arvan, 346*f*
    Ascension, 74*f*
    Axis Mundi, 122*f*
    Brasilia, 360*f*
    Breezy, 252*f*
    Brief Eulogy, 31*f*
    Canyon, 305*f*
    Carezza, 64*f*
    Catch the Breeze, 250*f*
    Cats & Dogs, 353*f*
    Celeste, 105*f*
    Celeste: Theme and Variations, 113*f*
    Celestial: In Memoriam ABM, 141*f*
    Ceremonial, 21*f*
    Charanga, 38*f*
    Chorale, 53*f*
    Chroma, 276*f*
    Cloverleaf, 215*f*
    Cloverleaf Piper, 217*f*
    Composure, 271*f*
    Constanze, 230*f*
    Cradle, 68*f*, 69*f*
    Crossed Albers, 294*f*
    Cycle of Heartbreak, 47*f*
    Distribuzione, 127*f*
    Dodecahedron, 163*f*
    Double Valtorna, 301*f*

compositions (*cont.*)
    Driven, 34*f*
    Driven Forward, 35*f*
    Easy Easy, 77*f*
    Émile, 48*f*
    Empty Nest, 201*f*
    Envelope, 206*f*
    Escalator, 37*f*
    Eulogy, 32*f*
    Fingers, 18*f*
    Forest Stone, 131*f*
    Geek, 154*f*
    Gemini, 348*f*
    Grace, 134*f*
    Heartbreak: Triptych, 80*f*
    Hello Hemiola, 23*f*
    Higher Simplicity, 14*f*
    Horn Call, 303*f*
    Hymn to the Pedal, 129*f*
    I Love Albers, 276*f*
    I Plead with Thee, 71*f*
    Im Nebel Gesehen, 102*f*
    Im Nebel Schwach Gesehen, 103*f*
    In Estonia, 92*f*
    Iocus, 265*f*
    Janus, 67*f*
    Jumping Frog, 39*f*
    Juventud, 40*f*
    Kaliště, 352*f*
    Klangbild I, 302*f*
    Klangbild II, 327*f*
    Light and Shadow, 194*f*
    Little Chorale, 52*f*
    Little Waltz, 62*f*
    Love Left, 205*f*
    Love Right, 207*f*
    Mahleriana, 321*f*
    Mano Sinistra, 324*f*
    Marrakesh, 98*f*
    Mikro, 205*f*
    Minor Albers, 277*f*
    Muster, 51*f*
    Mysterium, 20*f*
    Nadia, 167*f*
    Nancarrow's Day Off, 357*f*
    Nonus, 261*f*
    Not Too Easy, 78*f*
    Obsedanta, 197*f*
    Octane, 315*f*
    Octaviana, 266*f*
    Octavus, 261*f*
    Odd Man Blues, 245*f*
    Pacific Sunrise, 139*f*
    The Party, 209*f*
    Pentagram, 27*f*
    Piper, 216*f*
    Primus, 256*f*
    Promenade, 17*f*
    Quartus, 258*f*
    Quest, 267*f*
    Quintus, 258*f*
    Remorse, 202*f*
    Respect, 195*f*
    Rising Light, 286*f*
    Secundus, 257*f*
    Seesaw of Heartbreak, 242*f*
    Seesaw: Horse & Rider, 86*f*
    Seksy Sesky, 24*f*
    Septimus, 260*f*
    Sergei, 187*f*
    Sergei's Right, 189*f*
    Sergei's Warm-up, 187*f*
    Serpentipedi, 264*f*
    Sextus, 259*f*
    Shapeshifter, 350*f*
    Sharp Neighbor, 277*f*
    Simplicity, 13*f*
    Skend, 263*f*
    Stroll, 16*f*
    Sustenance, 45*f*
    Tallinn, 349*f*
    Tally Up, 25*f*
    Tertius, 257*f*
    Thimble, 199*f*
    Three of Eight, 29*f*
    Together Apart, 91*f*
    Transfiguration, 361*f*
    Trelliswork, 313*f*
    Trivium, 15*f*
    Tuba Mirum, 297*f*
    The Twelve, 220*f*
    The Twelve Crying Princes, 178*f*
    Valtorna, 300*f*
    Vázlat, 355*f*
    Venus Rising, 362*f*
    Waltz for Anni, 290*f*
    Yale Key, 288*f*
    Zwölf, 292*f*
constraint, 187, 195–97
counterclockwise journey, 147, 149, 155–60, 156*f*, 162, 166, 170, 173, 177, 218, 233, 351
counterweighing pinkies, 10*f*
counting, 21–29
    five-beat count, 26*f*
    hemiola, 22, 23*f*, 24*f*
    three plus three plus two, 22, 28*f*, 29*f*
crossing hands, 88–93, 191–95, 214, 219–20, 231, 294*f*

"Dialogue" (musical archetype)
    anchoring thumbs, 10*f*
    chord sequences, 12–19
    comfort and control, 11*f*

counterweighing pinkies, 10f
counting, 21–29
five-beat count, 26f
hemiola, 22, 23f, 24f
musical ambiguity, 11f
sonic textures, 19–21
three plus three plus two, 22, 28f, 29f
drone, 96, 121, 130, 231, 314, 319, 320, 345, 351

Echo (mythological character), 329–30
enveloped fingering, 206

feel-good tools, 87
fermata, 87, 99, 138, 177, 206, 211, 269, 298f
fingering, 12, 13, 16, 17, 18f, 19f, 44, 49, 50f, 51, 85, 99, 101, 121, 175f, 177, 210, 218, 233, 269, 274, 279, 283, 297, 332, 359
enveloped, 206
and intervals, 53–54
mirrored, 187
and nested hands, 200

germinating seed, 29, 36, 41, 138, 256, 257, 299
gesture, 8, 10, 11, 44, 59, 85, 94, 104, 109, 117, 182, 191, 203–7, 214, 227, 228, 297, 298, 299, 304, 332–33
crawler, 183f
crossing hands 191–95, 214, 219–20, 231, 294f
enveloped fingering, 206
nested thumbs, 200, 201f
passing thumbs, 204–6
speaking and singing thumbs, 198–202
stacked thumbs, 202
gradations, 64, 104, 109, 138, 191, 202, 214, 308

harmonic series, 117–22
in "Celeste," 123f
drone, 121
first 16 harmonics, 120f
hearing the harmonics, 118f
homework, 124–25
Mixolydian mode, 312f
sympathetic resonance, 118f
transposing, 125f
"Heartbreak" (musical archetype)
fingerings, 44, 49, 51
intervals, 53–55
note groupings, 56–58
SATB, 49f
singing thumbs, 48f
tonal and modal, 63–65
vertical and horizontal journeys, 48–53
voicing, 76f
hemiola, 22, 23f
"Horn Call" (musical archetype)
acoustic sensitivity, 306f
cluster, 304f
and drone, 320f
and fermata, 298f
and fortissimo, 298
harmonics, 310f
note groupings, 299f, 301f
sympathetic resonance, 304f

improvisation, 21, 29, 30, 44, 59–63, 64f, 99, 129, 140, 169f, 241, 261, 275, 301, 314, 345, 347, 353
and the circle of fifths, 169f
and constraint, 195–97
improphobic, 1
Interaction of Color, 284
interpretation, 44, 46–47, 101, 107, 173, 180–81, 233, 319, 320
"Intertwining" (musical archetype), 255f, 255
building blocks, 256–60
catalog of building blocks, 256f
dominant and tonic, 261f
mix and match, 261–68
transposition, 269–71
intervals, 1, 8, 46, 53–55, 99, 119, 130, 210, 214, 231, 233, 340, 359
enharmonic, 154, 155, 155f

joinery, 87f
juxtaposition of compositions, 79
"Breeze and Catch the Breeze," 251–52
"Easy and Not Too Easy," 79
"Heartbreak: Triptych," 80f
"Horn Call Suite," 329–30

layers of the keyboard, 165f

Mahler, Gustav, 153, 319, 320
Mikrokosmos, 204
Mixolydian mode, 65, 215, 219–20, 275, 284, 285, 311, 312f
Mozart, Wolfgang Amadeus, 21, 153, 227, 229–30
mudra
changeability, 335
definition, 332–33
E-major scale fragment, 359
entry point into the maze, 345
left-hand mudra, 340–45, 347
stability and elasticity, 334–39
sympathetic resonance, 347f
three against two, 353–58
trampoline, 334
transformation, 350–52
musical ambiguity, 1, 11f, 46, 65, 107, 155, 261, 274, 275, 311, 334, 345

Nancarrow, Conlon, 356
nested thumbs, 200, 201f

note groupings, 22, 56–58
    in "Aloysia," 233f
    in "Celeste," 107f, 109
    in "Heartbreak," 57f, 58f
    in "Tuba Mirum," 299f
    in "Valtorna," 300

pedaling, 19, 31, 51, 109, 121, 138, 140, 191, 272, 305, 308, 310, 314, 320, 334, 342, 349, 359
    "Hymn to the Pedal," 129
    una corda, 326
phobia, 353
Plato, 363–64
posture, 94, 108–9, 123, 191, 203, 213, 298, 332

resonance, 88, 98f, 111, 118, 124, 130, 195, 283–84, 299, 304f, 329–30, 347f
    and the harmonic series, 118f
    and voicing, 126–28
rewriting, 16, 48, 49, 105, 162, 228, 347

SATB, 48
"Seesaw" (musical archetype)
    bounce, 94–95
    challenges, 99–103
    feel-good tools, 87
    and joinery, 87f
    and poise, 94
    and rhythm, 85
simplification, 36, 150, 231
sonic sculpting, 140–46
sympathetic resonance, 88, 98f, 118f, 138f, 195f, 272, 273f, 304f, 347f

tendency tones, 96–99, 162
The Three Musketeers, 182
three against two, 353–58
thumbs
    anchoring, 10f, 33f, 43–44
    intelligent and adaptable, 13f
    intelligent and singing, 65–72
    nested, 200
    passing, 204
    speaking and singing, 198–202
    stacked, 202
    sustaining, 91, 92, 349
trampoline, 11, 94, 210, 334f
transposition, 88–93, 102, 126, 160, 169–81, 187, 218, 255
    and "Albers," 274, 275f, 279–81
    and "Aloysia," 233
    and "Celeste," 170
    and "Dialogue," 175
    enharmonic, 282–84
    and "In Estonia," 173
    and the harmonic series, 124
    and "Heartbreak," 177
    and "Intertwining," 269–71
    by thirds, 279–81, 281f

variation, 29–42, 59–63, 60f, 88–93, 89f, 111–16, 185f, 187, 190f, 196, 232f, 233, 275–78, 284, 299, 301
    "Celeste: Theme and Variations," 113f, 173
vertical and horizontal journeys, 48–53
Vivaldi, Antonio, 153
voicing, 68, 76, 126–28

Weber, Aloysia, 227
Weber, Constanze, 229–30

Printed in the USA/Agawam, MA
August 7, 2023

814142.052